OTHER BOOKS BY WILLIAM I. KAUFMAN

The Art of India's Cookery

The Sugar Free Cookbook

The Art of Creole Cookery

The Wonderful World of Cooking Series:
    Near East—Far East
    Caribbean—Latin American
    Northern European
    Southern European

Cooking with the Experts

The Thos. Cook & Son Pocket Travel Guides:
    Cook's Pocket Travel Guide to Europe
    Cook's Pocket Travel Guide to the West Indies

It Pays to Finish High School

Your Career in Television

Best Television Plays Volumes I, II, III, IV

How to Write for Television

How to Direct for Television

How to Announce for Television

How to Write and Direct for Television

THE COFFEE COOKBOOK

The Coffee Cookbook

BY WILLIAM I. KAUFMAN

Garden City, New York

DOUBLEDAY & COMPANY, INC.

1964

Illustrations courtesy of Comitato Italiano Caffè,
Dott. G. P. Ramasco-Vittor, President

Dedicated to
my wife Rosamond,
the light of my life and a great coffee maker

ACKNOWLEDGMENTS

THE COFFEE COOKBOOK has truly been a work of international co-operation. If by error I have forgotten to mention anyone, I trust that I will be forgiven.

Mr. John F. McKiernan, President; Mr. Joseph F. Drury, Director of Public Relations; Miss Sue Shaughnessy of the National Coffee Association; Mr. Paul Lang, Executive Secretary, The Green Coffee Association of New York City, Inc.; Mr. Samuel Matassa, Walter K. Lederhaus & Co.; Mr. Drachus, Weddle Tea Company; Mr. Mortimer H. Runkel, Mr. Eugene Davids, Mr. Donald Sperling of the Sprague & Rhodes Commodity Company; Mr. M. Zak, H. S. Fromme & Co.; Mr. Paul Eibert, Eibert Continental Coffee Co.; Mr. R. M. McGarvey, McGarvey-Atwood Coffee Co.; Mr. Robert D. Cords, Mr. Donald R. Keough of the Duncan Coffee Co.; Mr. H. C. Mueller, J. A. Folger & Co.; Mr. Jack Sassard, McCormick & Co., Schilling Div.

The Brazilian Coffee Institute, National Federation of Coffee Growers of Colombia, The National Coffee Association of Guatemala, The Coffee Industry Board of Jamaica, British West Indies.

Mr. J. Rault, General Secretary, Comité Français du Café; Mr. Paul Varon, Président, Syndicat du Commerce des Café Verts de Bordeaux; Mr. L. Gonin, le Secrétaire Général, Fédération Nationale des Syndicats du Commerce Ouest Africain; Mr. M. Soir, Secrétaire, Syndicat du Commerce des Cafés et Poivres au Havre; Mr. Walter Brangmo, Sveriges Kafferosteriers Förening, Stockholm; Mr. Ivar Mjønes, Norges Colonialgrossisters Forbund, Oslo; Mr. R. A. Krekel, Verein Deutscher Kaffee-Grosshandler Und Roster E.V.; Mr. F. Spoelstra, Stichting Koffiepropaganda Nederland, Amsterdam; Miss Helen MacKenzie, The Coffee Information Bureau, London; The Coffee Terminal Market Association of London; Mr. K. E. Webster, Secretary, The United

Kingdom Coffee Association Limited; Mr. Henrick Paulig, Oy Gustav Paulig Co., Helsinki; Mr. Giovanni Botteri, President, Associazione Commercio Caffè Droghe E Coloniali.

A special thanks to Dott. G. P. Ramasco-Vittor, President, Comitato Italiano Caffè for permission to use material from *Caffè Storici nel Mondo.*

The Coffee Brewing Institute for their material on making a good cup of coffee and Ellen Saltonstall for *The Coffee Newsletter* and its goldmine of historical and recipe information.

Foreword

To paraphrase the late poet, Robert Frost, there is one thing more exasperating than a wife who can brew coffee and won't. And that is a wife who can't brew coffee and will.

In the mind of the true lover of good coffee, there is no place in the kitchen of any self-respecting homemaker for the so-called "rule of thumb." Whatever that rule really means, it has been, at least in the case of coffee brewing, more honored in the breach than in the observance.

But lest we sound like a cantankerous coffee connoisseur, let us hasten to express our delight that, at long last, an accomplished writer has put the "secret" of good coffee between hard covers. And we are especially pleased that Mr. Kaufman has gone well beyond that achievement.

For this is no ordinary cookbook. In addition to spelling out his precise, step-by-step procedure for preparing the fruit product most often used in American homes—yes, it *is* coffee—the author has embellished his text with little-known but fascinating facts about the history of what has been called "the universal cup of cheer, the ambrosia of prince and peasant, the common denominator wherever good friends get together."

How many people know, for instance, that the beans from which we brew coffee beverages are the "seeds" of a ruby-red cherry that is the fruit of a tree bearing evergreen leaves and blossoms as lovely and as fragrant as the jasmine? How many know that George Washington's chief steward owned one of America's early coffeehouses? Or who put the perk in the percolator? These and a hundred more "conversation pieces" are interestingly revived in Mr. Kaufman's book.

Whether you're a coffee lover or not, if you wish to have

at hand an authoritative guide for the correct preparation of the beverage and its varied uses in cooking, as well as a captivating discourse on its origin, legends, and role in history and the arts, then Mr. Kaufman's work belongs on your bookshelf. Better make it a shelf close to the stove, for you'll be using it often.

JOHN F. McKIERNAN
President, National Coffee Association

Contents

Introduction

Coffee is the *largest single* agricultural import in the United States. Each day 441 million cups are consumed. At most breakfast tables, "if the coffee tastes good, everything tastes good," a fact so significant in itself that no other argument is needed to prove the importance of all-out success in the preparation of a cup or pot of this delicious beverage.

THE COFFEE COOKBOOK originated in my love for a good cup of coffee, a curiosity of the legends and history of coffee, plus the constant amazement as to why there existed such a wide range in the quality of coffees served in homes and restaurants.

I began by investigating the different ways of coffee making, the use of different coffee makers, the degree of fineness to which the coffees should be ground, the methods of roasting, the preservation of ground coffee, and a study of the varieties and qualities of beans necessary to produce the best results.

Grown in different and widely separated parts of the world, in soils which vary greatly one from the other, it is only natural that there should be considerable difference in the quality, appearance, and flavor of various coffees. Nor is it strange that individual palates, accustomed to the taste of a particular variety or blend, should find it difficult to accept any but those with which they are most familiar. It is this difference in personal taste which makes it almost impossible for even the most expert coffee *maker* to satisfy every coffee *drinker*, to say nothing of satisfying the coffee *lover*, sometimes referred to as the "coffee fiend."

It must be noted however that there are some criteria that apply to all varieties in their selection and preparation which, if observed, will add greatly to the quality of the coffee and the satisfaction of the coffee drinker.

It is not my *cause célèbre* to attempt to convince anyone who prefers his coffee black that additions will make the brew more palatable. Whether it is served black, with cream, sugar, or milk, experience has demonstrated that good coffee solidifies friends. I firmly believe that coffee was created for man's sustenance and pleasure to the same degree as was wheat, or the other fruits of nature.

The great surprise and delight manifested by the Indians on the western plains upon first acquaintance with coffee is legendary and gives us an example of how stunning an affect this beverage has had in the past. Usually indifferent to new objects and tastes, they failed to restrain themselves over the flavor of coffee. It is a matter of record that they traveled several hundred miles in order to gratify their taste for this new drink and the story is told of how an Indian chieftain, dressed in a robe of great beauty, came in contact with a trader, who tried by every means to secure the coveted robe. At last their meeting terminated with the accustomed treat of coffee. It seemed as if his spirits had been roused by some unseen power. He pressed eagerly for more and, delighted at receiving a second cup, he threw upon the trader as an expression of his joy, the magnificent robe that money could not purchase.

Similar instances have taken place with the introduction of coffee into all countries where it is consumed, and if today there are people who do not find pleasure in lingering over a cup of delicious coffee, it is due probably to the fact that they have never been initiated to the experience of its full flavor.

It is therefore my purpose in THE COFFEE COOKBOOK to try to point out how a good cup of coffee should be made, to touch upon its interesting background, and to suggest in recipe form some of the many taste treats that may be prepared using *coffee* as one of the main ingredients.

WILLIAM I. KAUFMAN

THE COFFEE COOKBOOK

A Short History of Coffee Drinking

Coffee is a fruit similar to a Bing cherry, and the product, which is so familiar to us in our home use, is created by using the stone or seed of that fruit shrub called the "coffee tree." Familiar as we all are with coffee as a beverage, few of us ever imagine that it has a history worthy of special notice. When we drink coffee, we often feel a sense of renewed vigor, but we are seldom provoked enough by curiosity to find out who was its discoverer, where it first grew, and by what process the habit of coffee drinking comes to us.

The saga of the fragrant little berry is as exciting as its aroma is exotic. Coffee first became known to civilization when men awakened from the sleep of the Middle Ages. It was originally known as *qahwah*, an Arabic word meaning strength and derived from the Turkish word *qahveh*. Today, in countries where the drink is used, its name has been adapted to local pronunciation, but interestingly enough it maintains, with rare exceptions, a form similar to the Turkish word. Some interesting examples are:

Chinese	*kia-fey*	Russian	*kophe*
Dutch	*koffie*	Swedish, Danish	*kaffe*
Finnish	*kahvi*	Annamite	*caphe*
German	*Kaffee*	English	*coffee*
Greek	*kaféo*	French, Spanish,	
Hungarian	*kavé*	Portuguese	*café*
Malayan	*kawa*	Italian	*caffè*
Polish	*kawa*	Rumanian	*cafea*

Scientific Latin......*coffea*

For the beginning of this history of coffee drinking, Eastern legend tells us of the discovery of the berry by a dervish named Hadji Omer, who was driven out of Mocha in the year 1285. Out of the anguish of hunger, the dervish roasted some berries growing near his hiding place. Desperately he ate them to stay alive, and then steeped the roasted berries in water to quench his thirst. The infusion saved his life, and his persecutors, who had intended that he die of starvation, looked upon his preservation as a miracle. The former outcast was quickly recognized as a saint. There is little further mention of the subject until we read in the fifteenth-century manuscript written by Scheha Beddin Ben, an Arabian scribe, that a certain Mohammedan high priest, named Gema eddin of Aden, was the first to introduce the custom of coffee drinking to his countrymen around 1454. On a visit to Persia, he had observed the beverage being used as a medicine. When he returned to his home, he felt sick and experimented with a dose of the "black draught." He found it both curative and stimulating and used it from then on to counteract the torpor of his monks, whenever he found them asleep during their prayers. The authority of the mufti gave coffee such a reputation that at once it speedily came into general use.

At the same time, coffee also was said to have been carried by the dervishes of Ethiopia (who had used it as a beverage before recorded time) to Mecca, where the fame of the beverage extended to other nearby towns, and to Syria, Damascus, and Aleppo. It found such favor at Constantinople that coffeehouses were opened there shortly after 1550. The growing popularity of the coffeehouses brought about the gradual desertion of the mosques, and in defense the priests declared coffee to be a kind of charcoal prohibited by the Prophet's law. A series of restrictions were leveled against it. Nevertheless, the people continued to drink the brew, ignoring the efforts of the police. Coffee was taxed, and people continued to drink it in secret. Later, another mufti rose to power, who saw the business aspects of coffee to be a very remunerative item of government tax. Coffee once more came "above ground." Later, however, too much freedom of political discussion took place around the coffee table, and the Oriental coffeehouses were closed by the grand vizier. Nevertheless, coffee continued to be universally used, some persons taking even twenty small cups per day. It even became the custom for the poor to beg money for coffee.

How long coffee remained unadorned cannot be exactly determined. First the Arabians drank it as a concoction of coffee hulls and pulps soaked in cold water. Time passed and the process of brewing improved until the hot, dark drink was made from berries, hulled, roasted, ground into a powder, and boiled in water without additives. But by the sixteenth century, the Turks were experimenting with spices. Sometimes they would boil the brew with cinnamon and cloves and add a drop of essence of ambergris when serving. It is doubtful that they even considered adding sugar to the beverage, but when the custom of coffee drinking passed from the "City of the Sultan" to Western Europe (where it is believed to have been introduced into Venice in 1615, and into Marseilles in 1644) the notion of sweetened coffee took hold. During the later part of the sixteenth century, European travelers discovered the beverage of the East aromatic and pleasantly stimulating, but far too bitter. Disdainfully, the Turks watched the visiting Westerners sugar the thick black brew in which they took such pride. Eventually, however, Turkish coffeehouse owners yielded to European inclination and began brewing coffee and sugar together. According to the writings of the German botanist Johann Vesling on the subject of the patrons of Cairo's three thousand coffeehouses, "some did begin to put sugar in their coffee to correct the bitterness of it, and others made sugar plums of the berries." The tremendous social stir that coffee drinking created in Europe brought the supply of sugar out of the apothecary's shop, where it was sold by the ounce at that time, and into the province of the grocer.

About the year 1669, Suleiman Aga, the Turkish ambassador to the court of Louis XIV at Paris, brought the beverage into high fashion at a series of diplomatic coffee parties. "The brilliant porcelain cups," wrote Disraeli some two centuries later, "in which it is poured . . . the napkins fringed with gold, and the Turkish slaves on their knees, presenting it to the ladies, seated off the ground on cushions . . . turned the heads of the Parisian *dames*."

Coffee became a subject of general conversation and a café was opened in 1671 in Paris by an Armenian named Pascal. It was not a successful venture, however, because of the intermingling of the classes. A few years later, Procope, a Florentine, known as an arbiter of taste in such matters, opened a splendid saloon in which only the *haute monde* of Paris gathered. The move was an unquestionable success. His patrons included a poor artillery officer named Napoleon Bonaparte. Soon the café became the meeting place of the most renowned wits, artists, and philosophers of France— Rousseau, Voltaire, and many others. Other cafés were opened, the most noted of which were the Café des Mille Colonnes and the Café Turc, both of which glittered with exotic Eastern ornamentation and opulent Oriental décor.

The high favor to which coffee rose is reflected by the fact that $15,000 a year was later expended to supply the daughters of Louis XV of France with the beverage; and in Germany, at the same time, the Elector of Brandenburg had a book written about coffee which he distributed to the populace. In 1714, the magistrates of Amsterdam presented Louis XIV with a coffee tree. It was planted in the Royal Gardens. A small seedling of this plant was taken secretly by a certain M. de Clieu to the island of Martinique, the French West Indian possession. After a treacherous voyage so rough and so prolonged that De Clieu had to divide his drinking water with the plant to keep it alive, he succeeded in planting the tree, from which such an immense progeny has sprung that at the outbreak of the Revolution, it was estimated that Martinique furnished no less than 80 million pounds of coffee per year to quench the French thirst for this beverage, irrespective of a liberal supply of coffee which they also imported from the East.

Indeed, so taken up with thoughts concerning this brew were the French that they were responsible for discovering that coffee did not need to be boiled but that it could be brewed by steeping. In 1755, they abandoned boiled coffee altogether to perfect what is today considered the "drip method." For four hundred years prior to that time everyone had a different notion about the best way to boil coffee, and it is interesting to know that the first percolator was invented by a Frenchman named Jean Baptiste de Belloy, whose first apparatus was little more than a drip pot without any pumping action. A long series of patents and variations came before the invention of the bubbling percolator we use today. De Belloy invented his percolator in about 1800. His principle had boiling water filter through ground coffee, held in suspension by a perforated metal or porcelain grid. The incomparable gastronomist, Brillat-Savarin, in his "Seventh Meditation," said of this new invention: "I have tried, in the course of time, all methods. Of all those which have been suggested to me up to today [1825], and with full knowledge of the matter in hand, I prefer the De Belloy method. . . ."

Although the De Belloy percolator was never patented, it moved Count Rumford, an American-British scientist and administrator who went to Paris to make a study of scientific coffee making, to produce an improved version of De Belloy's pot. Rumford was a great advertiser, and for this reason he, rather than De Belloy, is credited with the invention of the first percolator, though certainly his idea of compressing the coffee in a filter compartment and preventing agitation of the grounds by the water was an important contribution to the efficiency of coffee making. Rumford's percolator, perfected in Paris about 1806, was introduced to London in 1812, accompanied by a lengthy essay entitled, "The Excellent Qualities of Coffee and the Art of Making It in the Highest Perfection."

Several men experimented with different sorts of mechanisms through the years. In every case, it was their main objective to heat the water and brew the coffee in one operation. In a series of patents granted to a Frenchman named Laurens for the first pumping percolator, a device in which the water, lifted by steam pressure through an exterior tube, dripped slowly over the coffee; and to Jacques-Augustin Gandais, a Parisian jewelry manufacturer who invented a more practical method in which the water was raised through the handle of the pot and sprayed over the ground coffee, progress finally led to the year 1827 in which Nicholas Felix Durant patented a percolator equipped with an inner tube to raise the boiling water and spray it repeatedly over the coffee. Thus it was M. Durant who at long last gave us the percolator as we know it today.

In 1876, that New Englander John Bowman presented the American public with a domestic version of the pumping percolator, which filled American kitchens with the jolly sound of the "perk."

But let us return to our history. We have seen how the fashionable use of the brew in high society popularized the drink in France in the early 1700s. A similar interest seems to have taken hold in England. From the writing of Sir Henry Blount, who visited Turkey in 1634, we read: "The Turks have a drink called cauphee, made of a berry as big as a small bean, dried in a furnace, and beat to a powder of a sooty color, in taste a little bitterish, that they seethe and drink, hot as may be endured. It is good at all hours of the day, but especially at morning and evening, when to that purpose they entertain themselves two or three hours in cauphee houses, which, in Turkey, abound more than Inns and ale-houses with us. . . ."

Notwithstanding the opposition and prejudice which prevailed against the beverage for nearly a score of years after its first introduction, coffeehouses continued to increase in London and other large cities of England. All classes frequented them—literary men and artists, businessmen and social lions of fashion—each choosing a house proportional to his rank.

On the authority of Oldys, the antiquary, "the first use of coffee in England was known in 1657, when Edwards, a Turkish merchant, brought from Smyrna to London, Pasqua Rosee, a Ragusan youth, who prepared this drink for him every morning. But the novelty thereof drawing too much company to him, he allowed his said servant, with another of his sons-in-law, to sell it publicly, and they set up the first coffeehouse in London in St. Michael's Alley, Cornhill. They separating, Pasqua kept in the house; and he who had been his partner obtained leave to pitch a tent, and sell the liquor in St. Michael's Churchyard."

Aubrey, the Boswell of his day, says in his *Anecdotes*, to further tell the story, that the partner of Pasqua was one Bowman, who took an apprentice Paynter. Paynter learned the mystery of coffee making and soon set up for himself. Not long after this coffeehouses became numerous. An animated controversy was kept up about coffee and coffeehouses during the sixteenth and seventeenth centuries, with opposition coming from the ladies, who were excluded. In spite of this, coffee soon became the favorite drink in England and the shops which sold it became places of general resort. In 1675, some attempts were made by proclamation to close the coffeehouses but the government soon found that they had gone too far, for the coffeehouses had become the chief organs of public opinion and the headquarters for all the news of the day, and the English would not be robbed of their rights in this direction, and, in fact, were busy making innovations in the drink by adding sugar candy and even mustard to the brew. In other countries, other additives were coming into use also.

In 1691, Angelo Rambaldi reported in his *Ambrosia Arabica*, that the Italians liked cloves, cinnamon, sugar, and ambergris in their coffee. In 1660, the Dutch Ambassador to China made the first reported trial of coffee with milk, in imitation of Chinese tea with milk, and thereby unwittingly launched a custom which would one day gain almost universal acceptance. Naturally, coffee traveled to the New World and nowhere were its influences as deeply felt as in the old French market of New Orleans, where from the earliest time, it was conveniently distributed from early morning until nearly noon by the busy coffee vendors, plying their ware amongst the maze of stalls. It was served steaming hot, in the cleanest cups, with the best kinds of sugar. European, Creole, New Englander, men of the West and men of the Orient mingled in a mixture of the rude and refined, discarding all artificial distinctions in the very act of drinking in the crowded market, standing in the open street.

In the East, the coffeehouses of New York are intimately associated with the city's history. Early records show that in 1643, Martin Krigier built a tavern on what is now Broadway, near the north end of Bowling Green. It soon became the resort of the fashionable men of the day and was at times the headquarters of the Dutch governor, William Kieft. In after years, the King's Arms Tavern was built on the same site. During the excitement before the Revolution, it was known as Burns's Coffeehouse, and used for the meetings of merchants and the associations of "Liberty Boys." On the thirty-first of October, 1765, the merchants who were engaged in the importation of English goods met there and resolved to import no more goods from England until the Stamp Act was repealed. Two hundred merchants signed the resolutions. During the Revolution Burns's Coffeehouse became the headquarters of British General Gage. It remained a coffeehouse for many years until finally, in the year 1860, it was purchased for the making of a freight depot.

Perhaps the most famous coffeehouse in New York was the City Tavern. It was built in the early part of the eighteenth century by the De Lancey family and still stands as the Fraunces Tavern on the southeast corner of Broad and Pearl streets. Originally it was used as the De Lancey's town house. But in January 1762, the property was bought by Samuel Francis, or, as he later signed his name, Fraunces, who had won an enviable reputation as the former proprietor of the Masons' Arms, near Bowling Green and the Vauxhall Gardens in Greenwich Street. Fraunces opened the coffeehouse on Broad Street as a tavern under the sign of "Queen Charlotte." In 1765, he retired and the coffeehouse knew a series of changing owners until 1770, when Fraunces took possession once again. The coffeehouse enjoyed a large share of business. The societies met there, the chamber of commerce held its monthly meetings there until it secured a room of its own, but Fraunces' main fame came from the large dinner parties he catered during the evenings of the winter for the "Social Club," on the rolls of which appeared many well-known names. The club was broken up in 1775. In 1789, Fraunces, or as he was sometimes called, "Black Sam," became the chief steward in George Washington's presidential household.

The celebrated Tontine Coffee House, stood on the northwest corner of Wall and Water streets. Started in 1792, it was the scene of many events in the history of trade. The Merchants' Exchange made its home there, when 120 leaders of the business community purchased the property and formed the Tontine Association, designed to provide a central location for the business community in a place where they could assemble to discuss the probable results of their business projects. During their leisure, they could take a cup of coffee without walking the long distances to their homes on State Street, Bowling Green, and the lower part of Green-

The Tontine Coffee House, established in 1792 by
New York merchants.

wich Street. These merchants acted as the joint board of di-
rectors of the Tontine Association, which served as a founda-
tion for the formation of the New York Stock and Exchange
Board, which met in the building until 1827. Since it had
been stipulated in the original agreement of the Tontine Association that the house was to be kept and maintained as a
coffeehouse, the members could do little to change its status
until the year 1834 when, with the permission of the courts,
the house was rented for general business offices.

With this transaction, the era of the coffeehouse dimin-
ished in the city of New York for more than a century, but
interest in coffee and the process of making it continued to
fascinate the minds of men, and in 1840, Robert Napier, a

Scottish marine engineer, invented a vacuum machine to make coffee by distillation and filtration. Although he never patented his device, he directed its manufacture thirty years later in Glasgow at the works of Thomas Smith and Sons. His coffee maker was patterned after the French double-glass "balloon" percolator, designed many years before, and was the introductory step in the appearance of the vacuum coffee maker.

Even though office buildings and exchanges exist for the conduct of business, and the formation of clubs has taken care of the social needs of the business community in general, the recent decade has seen the rebirth of the coffeehouse tradition. The coffeehouse as a place in which to relax and exchange ideas has been revivified, and, throughout our major cities, charming spots may be found which harbor the sound of restful, unhurried conversations and the aromas of coffees from many lands, brewed in many styles—and universally savored, while across the back yards of the nation waft the sounds of America's invitation to friendship, "How about coming over for a cup of coffee?"

Coffee–From Tree to the Perfect Cup

The coffee tree is really not a tree at all. It is a universally important shrub, temperamental as a prima donna, that must be carefully pampered. It cannot tolerate wide temperature variations, endure even a mild winter by our standards, or suffer too much direct sunlight. It thrives best protected by taller shade trees in the temperate climates of the tropics and subtropics.

Raising a coffee crop requires many hours of patient, painstaking work. The coffee planter generally begins with seedlings, which he sows and tends in nursery beds for about a year until they are about twelve inches high. They are then transferred to plantation ground and placed in shallow holes eight to twelve feet apart.

The oldest plant in cultivation and the most widely used is the species *Coffea arabica*, although the planter also may utilize *Coffea liberica* and *Coffea robusta*, two other species which have become important in creating hybrid plants.

The coffee plant is individual and temperamental, some trees growing well at sea level—others needing heights as high as 6000 feet. They vary in their height from six to thirty feet and must have a soil porous enough to provide good drainage, but still rich in potash. Best results are achieved when the plants can get their requirement of seventy inches of annual rainfall, evenly spread out during the year. The planter is dedicated to supplying the coffee tree with water, drainage, shelter from high winds, burning sun, formidable pests, and diseases. He must feed it, weed it, and prune it regularly during the laborious three to five years which he endures between seeding and fruition. Delicate, snowy-white blossoms herald the final stages of development. If all goes well during the next two months, these blossoms are replaced by green coffee cherries, which ripen over the space of another six or seven months to a rich, dark, reddish black, until at last, they are ready for picking!

When the coffee cherries are ripe, whole families turn out to hand-pick the harvest. Some trees bloom several times a year, showing green and ripe cherries simultaneously with blossoms. Only the fully ripened cherries are selected for plucking—a job as yet impossible for a machine. If the season, the botanical strain, and the planter's luck are good, a six-year-old tree can produce anywhere from one to twelve pounds of green coffee.

The picked coffee cherries must be cleaned of all sticks, leaves, and other residues and then "cured." The heart of each cherry contains two seeds (or beans). During the curing process, the fruity pulp is discarded and only the beans, which become the coffee as we know it, are retained.

In countries where water is limited, the "dry" method of curing is used. For three weeks the cherries are spread in the sun and raked by plantation hands who turn them several times a day to insure uniform evaporation of the moisture, after which the hulls are removed by threshing and pounding in a mortar or by modern hulling machines. In countries where there is a good water supply, the planter uses the "wet" method, which is less time consuming. The cherries are soaked overnight in large tanks, following which pulping machines remove the softened outer skins. The beans are relieved of their gummy coating by a fermentation process, and then they are thoroughly washed and dried. To remove the thin, parchmentlike, whitish skin which remains after curing, the beans are polished by revolving cylinders. They are air blasted to extract dust and size graded by automatic sorters. Discolored or defective beans are carefully removed by skilled workers who inspect the crop, and the long, six-year growing process is complete.

More than half of the coffee growers' wares find their way by export to the shores of the United States, where the green beans are blended, roasted, and packed. Few people realize that nearly every cup of coffee they drink has been brewed from a blend of many coffees—a mixture of coffees chosen for specific qualities, such as aroma, body, acidity, or flavor, and combined. Today, almost all marketed coffees are blends, but in the early 1600s when Europe was introduced to the brown brew, only the pure product of Arabia existed. After the coffee plant had been carried to other lands, the French Martinique coffees, the Dutch Java coffees, and the English coffees from India were all used in their purest form. In the early nineteenth century, improved roasting and brewing equipment began to show coffee experts the true value of "flavor." They started to experiment with the mixing of varieties, when it became evident that no *single* coffee, no matter how delectable, could contain all the flavor qualities brought out by blending coffees together.

The creation of a new blend uses only coffees available in quantity at competitive price. *Flavor* and *cost* are the two factors that control the success of the blend created from an overwhelmingly wide choice of bean grown in South America, Central America, Mexico, Hawaii, the West Indies, Africa, Asia, and the South Sea Islands. Choosing such coffees is a complex affair. Coffee beans are distinguished by places or port of origin, or by the country in which they are grown. They are further distinguished by grade, sometimes as many as nine different ones. They are "washed" or "unwashed," referring to their method of curing. There are "old crop," "new crop," "high-grown central," and numerous others in this whirlwind of exotic titles. With his knowledge of coffee flavors, the roaster can anticipate the taste each coffee should possess when the bean is submitted to the "cup test."

Visualize two men bent over a large round table with a

revolving, Lazy Susan top. These are the tasters, who roast the beans, grind them, and measure out a nickel's weight of the precious coffee. Then they place the ground coffee in a cup and pour boiling water over the grounds. They sniff the aroma, stir the foam which forms atop the brew, and inhale the full fragrance. They sip the liquid from the spoon, savoring the coffee on the tongue. They test the coffee for body, smoothness, richness, mellowness, or acidity. They decide whether or not it is winy, neutral, or harsh. Finally, with force, they expectorate the coffee into the high brass spittoon set beside the table.

In the development of a new blend, coffee tasters do a major part of the work in testing countless samples of coffee, with an eye to selecting the best and deciding in what proportion they should be combined. Coffee-company executives work with the tasters testing results, discarding, retaining, changing, experimenting, criticizing, until at long last, together they achieve that which they set out to create, a new blend containing all the desirable qualities of bright flavor accent, body, color, aroma, and flavor.

The taster's job is not complete when a new blend is evolved; he must continue to sample every new shipment of beans, to see that the taste as well as the resulting blend remains constant. The quality of a particular coffee may differ too widely from season to season, or the bean may become unavailable in sufficient quantity. When this happens, the taster must find another coffee with similar characteristics to put in the blend. Only by this constant tasting process can the flavor and aroma characteristics of a *brand* of coffee remain perpetually consistent through the years.

Even taking into consideration that the coffee is a blend of the very best, a certain problem still exists. How to make that most desirable of things—the perfect cup of coffee. Blending is the romance of coffee, cooking it is the art. Some cooks know how to turn out "elixir," while others, using exactly the same coffee, make just a warm, brown drink. Strange—when, in all brewing methods, ground coffee and hot water are combined and kept in contact until a coffee beverage results. The true secret lies in knowing the exact proportions of coffee and water, the length of time contact should be maintained, for the particular kind of coffee maker used.

Here are some hints from the Coffee Brewing Institute for making the perfect cup of coffee in any coffee maker:

1. START WITH A THOROUGHLY CLEAN COFFEEPOT RINSED THROUGH WITH HOT WATER JUST BEFORE USING. Absolute cleanliness of the coffee maker is essential. Coffee contains oil, which forms an almost invisible film on the inner walls and assemblies of coffee makers. Unless this film is completely removed, it becomes rancid and will contaminate the flavor of all the succeeding brews. Coffee makers should be disassembled. Each part should be thoroughly scrubbed or brushed with a mild detergent or baking soda and water, and rinsed thoroughly. Above all, no metal scouring pads to cleanse the inside of your coffee maker, please!

2. USE FRESHLY DRAWN COLD WATER.

3. USE FRESHLY GROUND COFFEE. Buy only a supply large enough to last one week in the grind that is just right for your coffee maker—or grind your own.

4. USE THE FULL CAPACITY OF YOUR COFFEE MAKER. For smaller quantities, use smaller coffee makers. Never, in any case, is it wise to brew less than three quarters of your coffee-maker's capacity.

5. CONSISTENT TIMING IS IMPORTANT. When you find the exact timing that suits your coffee maker and the strength that suits your taste, stick to it to get uniform results.

6. NEVER ALLOW COFFEE TO BOIL. When it does, an undesirable flavor change takes place.

7. SERVE COFFEE AS SOON AS POSSIBLE AFTER IT IS BREWED. If you must serve it later, place the pot in a pan of hot water, or leave the coffee over a very low flame on an asbestos pad.

When measuring coffee, best results are obtained by using two level measuring tablespoons of coffee to each three-quarters standard measuring cup (6 fluid ounces) of water. Some cooks find it more dependable to use one Coffee Brewing Institute Approved coffee measure of coffee to each 6 fluid ounces of water.

HOW TO GET THE BEST COFFEE FROM YOUR FAVORITE POT

I. DRIP METHOD:

1. Preheat pot by rinsing with hot water.
2. Measure "drip grind" coffee into filter section. Place upper container in position.
3. Measure fresh boiling water into upper container and cover.
4. When dripping is completed, remove upper section. Stir brew to mix thoroughly before serving.

II. PERCOLATOR METHOD:

1. Measure fresh cold water into percolator. Place on heat until water boils. Remove from heat.
2. Measure "regular grind" coffee into basket.
3. Insert basket into percolator, cover, return to gentle heat, percolate slowly 6 to 8 minutes.
4. Remove coffee basket and serve.

III. VACUUM METHOD:

1. Measure fresh cold water into lower bowl. Place on heat.
2. Place filter in upper bowl. Add measured amount of "fine grind" or "drip grind" coffee.
3. When water boils, reduce heat or turn off electricity. With a slight twist to tighten, insert upper bowl into lower bowl.
4. Let water rise into upper bowl. Stir water and coffee thoroughly. In 1 to 3 minutes, remove from heat . . . exact time depending on grind and strength desired.
5. When brew returns to lower bowl, remove upper bowl, and serve.
6. If a cloth filter is used, it should be thoroughly rinsed after each use (no soap) and left aside immersed in cold water until used again.

IV. FILTERCUP COFFEE-EXTRACTOR METHOD:

1. Insert stainless steel disc in glass basket.
2. Insert filter into glass basket. Be sure stainless flow control disc is in place. Spoon in 1 standard coffee measure (2 level tablespoons) of "fine grind" coffee per cup.
3. Bring water to boil, remove from heat. When water stops bubbling pour just enough over grinds to wet and hold them down. Allow about one-half minute for saturation. Then slowly add hot water until the carafe is filled to the Extract Level Line (the 4-cup mark)!
4. Remove basket with filter-discard coffee grinds at your convenience. Fill carafe with hot water until you reach the mark showing the number of cups you need. Blend the extract with water by gently stirring for a moment.
5. Replace lid and serve.

COFFEE-MAKING CHART

Average 5½ oz. Servings	Level Measuring Tablespoons	Standard Measuring Cups of Water	Ounces of Water
2	4	1½	12
4	8	3	24
6	12	4½	36
8	16	6	48

FOR LARGE QUANTITIES OF COFFEE

20	½ lb. coffee	1 gallon water
40	1 lb. coffee	2 gallons water

Coffee in an Instant

The development of instant coffee in the past decade is undoubtedly one of the great success stories of our era. Contrary to popular opinion, this beverage has a history older than notions of the Civil War.

The first known reference to a soluble coffee preparation was made in 1838, when Congress substituted coffee for rum in Army-Navy rations. During the years following this, many experimentations were made, and in 1856, Gail Borden, inventor of evaporated milk, received a British patent on an extract made from milk and an essence of coffee, which yielded one cup of coffee to a half teaspoon of the liquid reconstituted with hot water.

In 1862, during the Civil War, Congress again took up the matter of soluble coffee and authorized the Secretary of War to supplement the armed forces' coffee ration with an "extract of coffee," such product to be "healthful, economical, and acceptable to the men." A solid cake, made by extracting and compressing the soluble parts of brewed coffee (invented it is believed by L. D. Gale), was submitted for their approval. One bite of this "coffee biscuit" was claimed to be the equal of a "half pint of strong coffee," though there is no record which tells us today whether Gale's substitute was ever actually used.

In 1899, Dr. Sartori Kato, a Japanese chemist who had invented soluble tea, came to Chicago and produced a soluble coffee, which he first sold at the Pan American Exposition in Buffalo in 1901. He later sold it in quantity to Captain

E. B. Baldwin, who found it to be completely satisfactory on the Ziegler Arctic Expedition of 1901–1902. Kato received U.S. patents on a coffee concentrate and a process for making same in August 1903.

G. Washington, who was born in Belgium of English parents and was a resident of Guatemala, was dining as usual in the shade of his orange trees, when he noticed that a brown powder had formed below the spout of his silver coffee-pot. Tasting the powder, he found it to possess real coffee flavor. This stimulated him to experiment over a period of several years until finally, with the help of American friends, he successfully reproduced the powder in quantities large enough for its introduction to the United States market in 1909.

However, it was World War I which brought soluble coffee to the front when the War Department requisitioned the entire output of Washington's company and that of other manufacturers for the use of American troops overseas. After trying to put it up in sticks, tablets, capsules, and other forms, it was finally the small envelopes of soluble coffee which were hailed by the military as "one of the most important articles of subsistence used by the Army."

Indeed, wartime emergency was a key factor in the production of instant coffee in World War II as well. Whereas in the years immediately preceding World War II, the market for soluble coffee was only ten million pounds per year, by comparison 257 million pounds of coffee concentrates were purchased for field rations by the United States Quartermaster Corps between 1942 and 1945. Since that time, the product has been refined and improved to a form which has given it complete acceptance in the American home.

How does this product achieve its "instant" form? In production, two basic steps are used: extraction and drying. To visualize how the extraction process works, imagine that you are facing a battery of giant, interconnected, coffeepots. In the beginning, roasted, ground coffee is brewed with purified water in the first of the containers. After a predetermined length of time at correspondingly correct temperature, the coffee liquid of the first pot passes through to the second container, in which there is additional fresh ground coffee. Each time the coffee is brewed under controlled conditions until all the coffee grounds are spent. Each time the liquid flows on to the next container . . . and the next . . . and so on, gathering strength as an extract until it is ready for the dryer. The manufacturers may select one of two different drying methods to procure instant coffee. One method produces a *powdered* instant coffee, the other a *bead* instant. To make the powder, coffee extract is fed onto a heated surface, all the moisture is evaporated and the dry material which forms is removed with a knife. It is then milled into a fine powder and packaged for consumption. Bead instant coffee results when the coffee extract is jettisoned by a spray nozzle through a current of hot air. The airflow evaporates the moisture, and the spray is dried into hollow, spherical particles ready for packaging.

Today these instant coffees are neither a novelty nor a vestige of wartime. They are an accepted household food staple from which one out of every five cups of coffee in the United States is made as naturally as though it had always existed.

HOW TO MAKE THE
BEST INSTANT COFFEE

TO MAKE A CUP OR INDIVIDUAL SERVING:

Place one teaspoon of instant coffee, more or less, according to strength desired, in a cup. Add boiling water. Stir. Cover cup with saucer for a few seconds before serving to develop flavor.

TO SERVE A SMALL GROUP:

To make 6 servings, pour one quart (4 measuring cups) actively boiling water on 6 teaspoons of instant coffee, more or less, according to strength desired. Stir or swirl gently in pot to assure a brew of even strength. Cover for a few seconds to insure development of full flavor.

TO SERVE A CROWD:

Use one 2-ounce jar of instant coffee to 6 quarts of boiling water for 32 servings of average strength. Pour measured water into large vessel, bring to a full rolling boil. Pour contents of 2-ounce jar of instant coffee into large server. Add boiling water. Stir to assure a brew of even strength. Cover for a few seconds to insure development of full flavor. Caution: Do not add instant coffee directly to boiling water . . . it will foam and overflow.

Iced Coffee

"CAFE MAZAGRAN!" Have you ever tasted it? It's iced coffee, concocted more than 125 years ago when French colonial soldiers stationed at Fort Mazagran, Algeria, found that drinking coffee syrup mixed with cold water made the intense desert heat more endurable. The vogue was carried back to Paris, where even today it bears the name of that spot where this tasty refreshment was developed out of desperation.

FOUR WAYS TO MAKE ICED COFFEE

QUICK:
Make your coffee double strength, using 1 standard measure (2 level tablespoons) of coffee to each 4 ounces of fresh, cold water. Pour over ice cubes. The extra-strength hot coffee compensates for the melting ice.

PRECOOLED:
Brew your coffee the regular way, using 1 standard measure of coffee to each 6-ounce cup of fresh, cold water. Cool in a tightly covered nonmetal container, no more than 3 hours. Pour over ice cubes.

COFFEE CUBES:
Make coffee cubes in the ice tray by freezing freshly brewed, regular-strength coffee instead of water. Use instead

of plain ice cubes, pouring hot, freshly brewed regular coffee over them. This gives the double-strength brew necessary for best results.

INSTANT:

Mix about twice the usual amount of instant coffee, according to taste, with a little water in each tall glass (this is based on 12-ounce cooler-type glasses). Then add ice cubes and fill with cold water.

Coffee Drinks Around the World

Coffee has often been called the "Universal Cup of Good Cheer." Taken from the oldest European traditions and customs for the making of coffee, some of these coffee recipes give you the opportunity of adding to your menus the French touch of *café au lait*, or the warm Irish charm of a good glass of "Irish coffee" into which honest Irish whiskey has been added.

I have included some recipes for the "weight-watchers" too. Although they cannot afford the high calories of pure cream, they can well enjoy a cup of *cappuccino*, adapted from the Italian borders, or a modern version of "Coffee Columbian," which calls for instant powdered milk or cream.

> *Last comes the beverage of the Orient shore,*
> *Mocha, far off, the fragrant berries bore.*
> *Taste the dark fluid with a dainty lip,*
> *Digestion waits on pleasure as you sip.*
>
> Pope Leo XIII—"Frugality"

CAFE AFRICAN

2 tablespoons instant coffee   2 cups boiling water
6 tablespoons sweet milk   Whipped cream
cocoa

Combine coffee, cocoa, and boiling water. Pour into two cups. Top with whipped cream. *Makes 4 servings.*

CAFE CACAO
(Brazil)

4 tablespoons instant coffee   ¼ cup crème de cacao
1½ cups boiling water   Whipped cream

Combine coffee, boiling water, and crème de cacao. Pour into two cups. Top with whipped cream. *Makes 2 servings.*

COFFEE COLUMBIAN

⅔ cup dry instant coffee   2 teaspoons instant coffee
  cream   1½ quarts strong coffee,
⅓ cup cold skim milk   chilled
1 teaspoon vanilla   1 pint coffee ice cream
1½ tablespoons sugar

Chill bowl and beaters in refrigerator for 15 minutes. Blend dry instant coffee cream, skim milk, vanilla, sugar, and instant coffee in chilled bowl. Whip at high speed with electric mixer until soft peaks form (3 to 5 minutes). Pour coffee into 6 tall glasses; top each with a scoop of ice cream and a mound of the whipped topping. *Makes 6 servings.*

CAFE AU LAIT
(France)

1½ cups strong, hot coffee
1½ cups hot milk

Using two pots, pour simultaneously into cups. *Makes 4 servings.*

IRISH COFFEE

Fine granulated sugar   *Irish whiskey*
Strong black coffee   *Heavy cream*

Into a warmed wine glass, place two teaspoons of sugar and fill glass about two thirds with hot coffee. Mix. Add about two tablespoons of Irish whiskey and float cream on coffee by carefully pouring over back of a silver spoon. *Makes 1 serving.*

ITALIAN COFFEE

4 standard coffee measures   *French- or Italian-roast*
(8 level tablespoons)   *pulverized coffee*
1½ cups water

A drip pot may be used, but a *macchinetta* is best. This coffee-making device consists of two cylinders, one with a spout, and a coffee sieve between them. Measure the coffee into the sieve. Put together with cylinder having the spout on top, and with measured water in lower cylinder. Place on heat and wait for small opening in lower cylinder to steam. Then remove from heat and turn the *macchinetta* upside down until all the brew has dripped through. Serve in demi-tasses or wine glasses with a twist of lemon peel and sugar, never with cream. *Makes 4 demitasse servings.*

CAFFE CAPPUCCINO

Combine equal quantities of steaming Italian coffee and steaming milk. Pour into Cappuccino cups and sprinkle with cinnamon and nutmeg. Serve with sugar.

CAFFE BORGIA

Combine equal quantities of steaming Italian coffee and hot chocolate. Pour into cups and top with sweetened whipped cream. Sprinkle with grated orange peel.

CAFE COINTREAU
(Italy)

1 tablespoon instant coffee
1½ cups boiling water

¼ cup Cointreau
2 thin strips of lemon peel

Combine coffee, boiling water, and Cointreau. Pour into two cups. Add one strip of lemon peel to each cup. *Makes 2 servings.*

ITALIAN COFFEE FOAM

4 egg yolks
4 tablespoons granulated
  sugar

10 tablespoons demitasse
  coffee (French- or
  Italian-roast)
2 tablespoons brandy

In the top of a double boiler, combine egg yolks, sugar, coffee, and brandy. Over hot, but not boiling water, whip with wire whisk until mixture is thick and light. Do not let mixture boil. Pour into decorative glasses and serve at once. *Makes 4 servings.*

COFFEE GRANITO
(*Italy*)

½ cup sugar
2 cups very strong, hot coffee

Combine sugar and coffee in saucepan. Stir until sugar is dissolved. Pour into a bottle. Allow bottle to cool. Place in freezer, turning from time to time in order that coffee doesn't freeze solid. When *granito* is poured it should be consistence of shaved ice. *Makes 4 to 6 servings.*

The Caffè Greco, still open in Rome, as it was in the time of Goethe.

CAPPUCCINO CUP
(*Italy*)

2 cups hot water   ¼ cup sugar
1 cup dry instant coffee   ¼ teaspoon nutmeg
cream   Chocolate curls
4 cups strong, hot coffee

Stir water and dry instant coffee cream together. Mix in coffee, sugar, and nutmeg. Pour into cups and garnish with chocolate curls. *Makes 8 servings.*

INSTANT CAPPUCCINO
(*Italy*)

1⅓ cups instant nonfat   ½ cup sugar
  dry milk crystals   2¾ cups boiling water
2 tablespoons instant coffee   Cinnamon
1 cup ice water

Mix instant milk crystals, instant coffee, and ice water together. Whip until stiff peaks form (4 to 6 minutes). Gradually add sugar, beating constantly. Gradually stir in boiling water. Serve topped with cinnamon. *Makes 6 servings.*

MEXICAN COFFEE

3 cups boiling water
1 cup freshly ground coffee
Milk

Pour water over coffee in drip pot. Keep pouring coffee back over coffee grounds twenty times. Pour coffee extract into bottle with tight top and chill. For each serving pour 1 cup milk into saucepan. Add 1 tablespoon of coffee extract. Bring to boil. Serve.

CINNAMON-STICK COFFEE
(Mexico)

2 cups boiling water
2 2-inch cinnamon sticks
4 teaspoons instant coffee

2 4- or 5-inch cinnamon sticks

Combine boiling water and two 2-inch cinnamon sticks. Cover and simmer for 5 minutes. Strain. Pour into two cups. Add 2 teaspoons coffee and one 4- or 5-inch cinnamon stick to each cup. *Makes 2 servings.*

TURKISH COFFEE

1½ cups water
4 tablespoons finely ground coffee
4 teaspoons sugar

Measure water into heavy saucepan. Add sugar and bring to a boil. Stir in coffee. Bring to a boil. Allow brew to froth up three times, then remove from heat. Add a few drops of cold water. Spoon some of the foam into each cup and pour in the coffee. *Makes 4 demitasses.*

HONEYPOT COFFEE
(Turkey)

½ cup water
1 tablespoon sesame seeds
1 tablespoon honey

3 tablespoons instant coffee

Combine water, sesame seeds, and honey. Bring to a rolling boil. Reduce heat. Cover and simmer for 5 minutes. Remove from heat. Add coffee. Strain into two demitasses. *Makes 2 servings.*

VIENNESE CHOCOLATE

1½ quarts strong coffee
⅔ cup chocolate syrup
2 teaspoons vanilla
⅔ cup dry instant
  coffee cream

⅓ cup cold milk
1½ tablespoons sugar
1 pint vanilla ice cream

Stir together coffee, syrup, and 1 teaspoon of the vanilla; chill. Meanwhile, chill bowl and beaters in refrigerator for 15 minutes. Blend dry instant coffee cream, milk, remaining vanilla, and sugar in chilled bowl. Whip at high speed with electric mixer until soft peaks form (3 to 5 minutes). Pour coffee mixture into 6 tall glasses; top each with a scoop of ice cream and a mound of the whipped topping. *Makes 6 servings.*

Some International Favorites

CAFE BRULOT

1 quart strong, black coffee
1 stick cinnamon
8 whole cloves
1 piece orange peel, 3 to
3½ inches long

1 piece lemon peel, 2½ to 3
inches long
6 lumps sugar
1 cup brandy
¼ cup Cointreau

Make black coffee, using 2½ tablespoons ground coffee to each cup water. Keep warm while mixing spices, orange and lemon peels, sugar, brandy, and Cointreau in a chafing dish. Heat. Ignite and stir with a ladle to dissolve sugar while flaming. Gradually stir in black coffee and continue stirring until flame ceases burning. Serve hot in *brûlot* cups. *Makes 8 servings.*

COFFEE GROG

SPICED BASE:

2 tablespoons butter
½ pound (½ package)
firmly packed brown sugar
Few grains salt

⅛ teaspoon cinnamon
⅛ teaspoon nutmeg
⅛ teaspoon allspice
⅛ teaspoon cloves

Cream butter. Add sugar slowly, while creaming. Add salt and spices. Blend thoroughly. This spiced base can be kept indefinitely in a covered container in the refrigerator.

GROG:

Put 1 teaspoon spiced-base mixture in each 6-ounce mug. Add a strip of lemon peel and another of orange peel. Measure in 3 tablespoons light rum and 2 tablespoons heavy cream. Fill mug with very hot coffee.

HOT MOCHA

2 *tablespoons sugar*
2 *tablespoons cocoa*
2 *teaspoons instant coffee*
1/16 *teaspoon salt*
2 *cups hot water*

2 *cups scalded milk*
2 *teaspoons pure vanilla extract*
6 *marshmallows*

Combine the first 4 ingredients in a saucepan. Blend in ¼ cup of water and boil 1 minute. Add hot milk and remaining boiling water. Heat 1 to 2 minutes. Stir in pure vanilla extract. Serve hot in coffee cups. Top with marshmallows. *Makes 6 servings.*

HOT MOCHA JAVA

4½ *cups hot coffee*
4½ *cups hot cocoa*
12 *marshmallows*

Combine coffee and cocoa. Reheat. Pour into cups or mugs and top with marshmallows. *Makes 12 servings.*

MOCHACHINO

1 cup dry instant coffee cream
2 cups hot water
½ cup instant sweet cocoa

2 cups strong, hot coffee
1 teaspoon grated orange peel
Orange-peel twists

Stir dry instant coffee cream into water. Blend in instant cocoa. Cook over low heat to serving temperature, stirring frequently. Add coffee and grated orange peel. Garnish with orange-peel twists. *Makes 4 to 6 servings.*

VIENNESE VELVET

1 quart vanilla ice cream
6 cups double-strength, hot coffee
Whipped cream

Place 1 large scoop of vanilla ice cream in each of 6 tall glasses. Pour hot, double-strength coffee carefully over ice cream until glass is about ⅔ full. Add a second scoop of ice cream and fill glass with coffee. Garnish with whipped cream, and add a sprinkle of nutmeg if desired. You will need long spoons for the first half of this dessert-beverage, but you will drink the latter half. *Makes 6 servings.*

Some U. S. Favorites

BREAKFAST COFFEE NOG

¼ cup dry instant
coffee cream
¼ cup instant coffee
¼ cup sugar

1 quart boiling water
4 eggs
1 teaspoon vanilla

Stir dry instant coffee cream, instant coffee, and sugar into water; cool thoroughly. Beat in eggs and vanilla. Chill. *Makes 4 servings.*

HALLOWEEN COFFEE

4 cups strong, hot coffee
2 medium unpeeled
oranges, sliced thin
Sugar to taste
½ cup heavy cream

2 tablespoons sugar
1 tablespoon grated orange
peel
Shaved unsweetened
chocolate

Pour hot coffee over sliced oranges. Let stand ½ hour. Strain. Reheat coffee, do not boil. Sweeten, if desired. Pour into 4 mugs. Whip cream; add 2 tablespoons sugar while whipping. Float on coffee. Garnish with orange peel and chocolate shavings. *Makes 4 servings.*

SLEIGH RIDES

4 squares (1 ounce each) unsweetened chocolate
4 cups strong, hot coffee
½ cup sugar
1 tablespoon vanilla

2 cups heavy cream, divided
Red sugar
Candy canes

Melt chocolate over hot water and add hot coffee and sugar. Stir until sugar dissolves. Remove from heat and add vanilla. Pour 1½ cups heavy cream into a bowl, add hot coffee mixture and beat with rotary beater until very foamy. Pour into mugs. Whip remaining cream and top each mug with a spoonful. Sprinkle with red sugar. Use one candy cane in each mug as a decorative and flavorful stirrer. *Makes 6 to 8 servings.*

COFFEE-BANANA MILK PUNCH

2 medium, fully ripe bananas
3 cups milk
¼ cup sugar
2 teaspoons instant coffee

1 teaspoon pure vanilla extract
Whipped cream for garnish

Slice bananas, mash and mix with ½ cup milk. Mix sugar with instant coffee and add. Stir in remaining milk and vanilla extract. Beat with a rotary or electric beater. Serve in tall glasses. Top with whipped cream. *Makes 1 quart.*

MOCHA MILK PUNCH

2 quarts skim milk
3 squares (1 ounce each)
  unsweetened chocolate
3 tablespoons instant
  coffee

¾ cup sugar
¼ teaspoon maple extract
2½ cups Cinnamon-
  Whipped Instant
  Crystals*

Combine skim milk, chocolate, coffee, and sugar in large saucepan. Cook over medium heat, stirring constantly, until chocolate is melted. Add maple extract; beat well. Stir in half of Cinnamon-Whipped Instant Crystals (given below); top with remaining whipped crystals. *Makes 6 servings.*

CINNAMON-WHIPPED INSTANT CRYSTALS*
Combine ½ cup instant nonfat dry milk crystals and ½ cup ice water in bowl. Whip until soft peaks form (3 to 4 minutes). Add two tablespoons lemon juice, 1 teaspoon vanilla, and ¼ teaspoon cinnamon. Continue whipping until stiff peaks form (3 to 4 minutes longer). Gradually add ¼ cup sugar.

ROYALE PUNCH

4 cups strong coffee
2 tablespoons powdered
  sugar

½ pint brandy
1 "fifth" domestic
  champagne

Combine coffee, sugar, and brandy; chill. Just before serving pour over ice in punch bowl. Add champagne. *Makes about 20 punch-cup servings.*

The Philadelphia *Journal* was born in this old Philadelphia coffeehouse.

SOUTHERN COFFEE PUNCH

2 *quarts strong, cold coffee*
1 *pint cold milk*
2 *teaspoons vanilla*
½ *cup sugar*

1 *quart vanilla ice cream*
½ *pint heavy cream,*
  whipped
Nutmeg

Combine cold coffee, milk, vanilla, and sugar in large bowl. Stir until sugar is dissolved. Chill thoroughly. At serving time, pour over ice cream in punch bowl and top with whipped cream. Sprinkle lightly with nutmeg. *Makes 15 to 18 punch-cup servings.*

VANILLA-COCOA PUNCH WITH COFFEE ICE CREAM

⅓ cup cocoa
⅓ cup sugar
¼ teaspoon salt
½ cup water

4½ cups milk
2 teaspoons pure vanilla extract
1 pint coffee ice cream

Combine first 4 ingredients in a saucepan. Mix well and bring to boiling point. Cook 2 minutes over medium heat. Stir in milk. Cook until hot, stirring constantly. Stir in pure vanilla extract and chill. To serve, pour in a 2-quart punch bowl. Float coffee ice cream over the top. Serve in punch cups. *Makes 8 to 10 servings.*

VANILLA-MOCHA PUNCH

1 quart freshly made strong, cold coffee
½ teaspoon ground cinnamon
1 teaspoon pure vanilla extract

¼ cup sugar
1 quart chocolate ice cream
1 cup heavy cream, whipped

Pour coffee into a punch bowl. Dissolve cinnamon in the pure vanilla extract and add to the coffee along with the sugar. Add half of the ice cream and stir until the ice cream is partly melted. Float remaining ice cream and whipped cream over the top. Serve in punch cups. *Makes 2 quarts.*

CAFE TROPICANA

4 cups strong, cold coffee Sparkling water
1 cup light cream Sugar syrup
1 teaspoon rum flavoring

Combine coffee, cream, rum flavoring. Chill. Pour into 6 tall glasses. Fill glasses with ice-cold sparkling water. Stir gently. Sweeten with syrup. *Makes 6 servings.*

CHILLED CAFE A LA CREME

Fill parfait glasses to the brim with chipped ice. Pour in strong, cold coffee, sweetened or not, filling glasses about two thirds full. If desired, add a dash of a liqueur, such as anisette, Cointreau, cognac, kümmel, Grand Marnier, maraschino, or white crème de menthe. Pour in plain, heavy cream almost to brim. Serve at once.

COFFEE-BANANA FLOAT

1 ripe banana 1 cup cold milk
1 cup strong, cold coffee 1 teaspoon vanilla
½ cup heavy cream 3 scoops coffee ice cream
2 teaspoons very fine sugar

Mash banana with fork or in an electric blender. Add coffee, cream, and sugar. Beat with rotary beater or in blender until thoroughly mixed. Add milk and vanilla. Mix well. Pour into 3 tall glasses. Add 1 scoop of coffee ice cream to each glass. *Makes 3 servings.*

COFFEE-BUTTERSCOTCH FOAM

6 tablespoons butterscotch   ½ pint (1 cup) coffee ice
topping   cream
4 tablespoons light cream   2 cups double-strength,
                              chilled coffee

Combine ingredients in electric blender or large bowl of electric mixer. Blend or beat until frothy. Serve at once in tall glasses. *Makes 3 servings.*

COFFEE CARDAMOM

1 quart strong, hot coffee   ⅓ cup cold skim milk
¼ teaspoon cardamom   1½ tablespoons sugar
⅛ teaspoon mace   1 teaspoon vanilla
⅔ cup dry instant coffee
cream

Stir together coffee, ⅛ teaspoon of the cardamom and mace. Keep hot but do not boil. Chill bowl and beaters in refrigerator for 15 minutes. Blend dry instant coffee cream with remaining ingredients in chilled bowl. Whip at high speed with electric mixer until soft peaks form (3 to 5 minutes). Serve Coffee Cardamom with the whipped topping. Sprinkle remaining cardamom on top. *Makes 6 servings.*

COFFEE-PEACH SHAKE

1 can (1 pound) sliced   ¼ cup water
cling peaches   1 cup light cream
2 teaspoons instant coffee   ½ pint vanilla ice cream

Put peaches, instant coffee powder, water, and cream in electric blender. Blend on high speed until thoroughly combined. Add ice cream about one fourth at a time, blending after each addition. If blender is too full, pour off some of the mixture; this can be returned later when all ice cream has been added. Serve in chilled glasses. *Makes about 4 servings.*

CREAMED CINNAMON COFFEE

4 cups strong, hot coffee
3 sticks cinnamon

Sugar or sugar syrup
½ cup heavy cream

Pour hot coffee over cinnamon sticks and let stand for about one hour. Remove cinnamon sticks and sweeten coffee to taste. Add heavy cream and chill. Pour over cracked ice in tall glasses and use cinnamon sticks as stirrers. *Makes 4 to 5 servings.*

CREAMY COFFEE FOAM

2 cups strong, cold coffee
½ teaspoon Angostura
bitters

½ cup heavy cream
Bottled cream soda

Combine coffee, bitters, and cream; divide among 4 decorative glasses. Add ice cubes. Fill glasses with cream soda. Stir gently to mix. If you prefer, use cold coffee and thoroughly chilled cream soda and dispense with the ice. *Makes 4 servings.*

DE-LUXE FROSTY MOCHA

2 teaspoons instant coffee
¼ cup boiling water
2 teaspoons sugar
1/16 teaspoon salt
2½ cups milk

2 teaspoons pure vanilla
extract
½ pint chocolate ice
cream

Dissolve coffee in boiling water. Chill, stir in sugar, salt, milk, and pure vanilla extract. Add ice cream. Mix well. Serve in tall glasses. *Makes 3 to 4 servings.*

DOUBLE-COFFEE ICE-CREAM SODA

½ cup Coffee Syrup*
½ cup heavy cream

1 quart coffee ice cream
Chilled sparkling water

In each of 4 tall glasses blend 2 tablespoons each Coffee Syrup and heavy cream. Add scoops coffee ice cream. Fill glasses slowly with sparkling water. Stir gently to mix. *Makes 4 servings.*

COFFEE SYRUP*

¼ cup instant coffee
½ cup hot water
2 cups light corn syrup

¼ teaspoon salt
2 teaspoons vanilla

Dissolve instant coffee in hot water. Blend in corn syrup and salt. Simmer 5 minutes. Remove from heat. Skim. Add vanilla. Cool. Store in covered pint jar in refrigerator. *Makes 2 cups.*

FROSTED COFFEE HAWAII

2 cups strong, cold coffee
1 pint softened coffee ice cream
1 cup chilled pineapple juice

Combine ingredients and beat thoroughly with a rotary beater or electric blender until the mixture is smooth and foamy. Pour into tall glasses. *Makes 4 to 5 servings.*

HOLIDAY MOCHA EGGNOG

2¼ cups boiling water
3 tablespoons instant coffee
1 cup sugar
6 eggs, separated
1 quart chocolate ice cream, softened

1 quart milk
1 pint heavy cream
2 teaspoons vanilla
1 square (1 ounce) sweet chocolate, shaved
Nutmeg

Combine water, coffee, and sugar; simmer for 3 minutes. Chill. Beat egg whites until stiff but not dry. Beat yolks until thick and lemon-colored; gradually pour in chilled coffee syrup. Beat in ice cream; stir in milk, heavy cream, and vanilla extract. Fold in egg whites. Pour into punch bowl; sprinkle with shaved chocolate and nutmeg. *Makes 25 servings.*

ICED VANILLA MOCHA

3 cups cold coffee
3 cups cold cocoa
1½ teaspoons pure vanilla
extract

Ice cubes
1 cup sweetened, whipped
cream

Combine first 3 ingredients. Place 2 ice cubes in each tall glass. Fill glasses with coffee-cocoa mixture. Top each with 2 tablespoons whipped cream. *Makes 6 to 8 servings.*

LA SHAKE FRANCAISE

1 tablespoon instant coffee
1 tablespoon boiling water
½ cup vanilla ice cream
⅓ cup crème de cacao

1 teapoon white crème de
menthe
6–7 ice cubes

Combine instant coffee and boiling water. Pour in blender. Add ice cream, crème de cacao, crème de menthe, and ice cubes. Cover blender and blend until ice is finely crushed, approximately 2 minutes. Serve in 5-ounce glasses. *Makes 4 servings or 2 cups.*

LUSCIOUS COFFEE FROSTED

½ cup instant nonfat dry
milk
½ cup ice water
¼ cup sugar

2 tablespoons instant
coffee
1 pint coffee ice cream,
slightly softened

Chill beater blades and small bowl of electric mixer. Measure instant dry milk into chilled bowl. Add ice water; blend. Beat at high speed until soft peaks form (about 5 minutes). Combine sugar and instant coffee. Add slowly, continuing to beat. Turn to low speed. Add ice cream, about a quarter of it at a time, beating after each addition until blended. Serve at once. *Makes 3 to 4 servings.*

PANAMA COOLER

2 *cups strong, cold coffee*   ½ *cup evaporated milk*
2 *ripe bananas*   1 *quart cream soda*

Combine coffee, bananas cut in chunks, and evaporated milk in electric blender or small bowl of electric mixer. Blend or beat until smooth and creamy. Divide equally among 6 tall glasses and fill glasses with ice-cold cream soda. Stir gently to mix.

Main Dishes

COFFEE

O, Boiling, bubbling, berry, bean!
Thou consort of the kitchen queen—
Browned and ground of every feature,
The only aromatic creature,
For which we long, for which we feel,
The breath of morn, the perfumed meal.

Arthur Gray (1902)
from "Over the Black Coffee"

MEAT BALLS PIEMONTE

2 pounds lean beef, ground
½ garlic clove, crushed
1 medium onion, finely chopped
¼ teaspoon each, savory, oregano, and paprika
2 teaspoons salt
1 cup bread crumbs
1 tablespoon prepared mustard
Dash Tabasco sauce

2 teaspoons Worcestershire sauce
Flour
4 strips bacon, cut into small pieces
1 cup strong coffee
½ cup Burgundy wine
½ cup water
1 teaspoon salt
1 teaspoon sugar
1½ tablespoons flour
1 cup dairy sour cream

Combine meat, garlic, onion, herbs, salt, crumbs, mustard, Tabasco and Worcestershire sauces; mix well. Form into approximately 2½ dozen balls. Dust with flour. Cook bacon until crisp and brown; remove from pan. Sauté meat balls in bacon drippings until lightly browned. Add coffee, wine, water, salt, and sugar. Simmer 15 minutes. Return bacon to pan. Stir in 1½ tablespoons flour, mixed smooth with ¼ cup cold water. Cook gently 5 minutes longer. Reduce heat. Garnish with dollops of sour cream. *Makes 6 to 8 servings.*

ROAST LAMB WITH COFFEE

1 5- to 7-pound leg of lamb
1 lemon, cut in half
Salt to taste
Freshly ground black pepper
4 tablespoons of instant or finely ground coffee
1 lemon, thinly sliced
4 cups double-strength coffee

Rub lamb with lemon halves. Sprinkle with salt and pepper. Place lamb on rack in open pan, skin side up. Add no liquid. Sprinkle top of lamb with instant coffee or finely ground coffee. Place lemon slices on top of coffee. Roast at 300° F. Allow 25 minutes per pound for pink lamb, 30 minutes per pound for medium lamb, and 35 minutes per pound for well-done lamb. During last hour of roasting pour liquid coffee over lamb every 15 minutes to baste. *Makes 8 to 10 servings.*

BARBECUED SPARERIBS

5 to 6 pounds spareribs, cut in serving pieces
1 cup strong coffee
½ cup molasses
¼ cup prepared mustard
1 tablespoon Worcestershire sauce
½ cup cider vinegar
Few drops Tabasco

Arrange spareribs one layer deep in large, shallow roasting pans. Combine remaining ingredients. Heat and stir until blended. Brush lavishly over ribs. Place in moderate oven (350° F) and bake, uncovered, 2½ hours, basting frequently with remaining sauce. *Makes 8 servings.*

The façade of the café, Le Trocope, a celebrated center of Parisian literary and philosophical life in the eighteenth and nineteenth centuries.

BEEF BRETONNE

4 tablespoons butter or
margarine
3 pounds round steak cut
in ¾-inch cubes
1 clove garlic, crushed
3 onions, sliced
4 tablespoons flour

½ cup Burgundy wine
½ cup water
2 teaspoons salt
½ teaspoon pepper
¼ teaspoon rosemary
¼ teaspoon oregano
1 cup strong coffee

Melt butter or margarine in deep frying pan or chicken fryer; add cubed steak; brown on all sides. Add garlic and onions; cook until onions are soft but not brown. Remove meat and onions from pan. Blend flour with butter remaining in kettle. Add wine, water, seasonings, and coffee. Stir until slightly thickened. Return meat and onions to kettle. Cover; bring to boil. Reduce heat and simmer 1½ hours, or until meat is tender. *Makes 6 servings.*

QUICK BOSTON BAKED BEANS

1 medium onion
½ teaspoon dry mustard
Salt and pepper
2 1-pound cans Boston-
style baked beans

½ cup molasses
½ cup strong coffee
½ cup boiling water
¼ pound fat salt pork

Peel onion and place in bean pot or deep casserole. Mix dry mustard with beans and add salt and pepper to taste. Combine molasses, coffee, and boiling water; pour over beans. Scrape pork rind; score with sharp knife. Bury pork in beans, leaving rind exposed. Bake in moderate oven (350° F), 1 hour. *Makes 6 to 8 servings.*

CHEESEBURGER PIE

2½ pounds lean beef, ground

2 cups soft whole-wheat bread crumbs

2 eggs

½ cup strong coffee

½ cup evaporated milk

1½ tablespoons instant minced onion

2 teaspoons seasoned meat tenderizer

1 teaspoon Worcestershire sauce

1 tablespoon prepared mustard

4 slices processed American cheese

Combine meat, bread crumbs, and eggs. Combine coffee, evaporated milk, and instant minced onion and let stand 10 minutes. Add to meat mixture with meat tenderizer, Worcestershire sauce, and mustard. Mix thoroughly. Pack into 10-inch pie plate. Bake in moderate oven (350° F) about 1 hour. Cut cheese slices in half, on the diagonal, and place around edge of pie. Place under broiler until cheese melts and browns. *Makes 8 to 10 servings.*

COFFEE-GLAZED HAM LOAF

2 pounds lean pork, ground

1 pound smoked ham, ground

1 cup soft bread crumbs

½ teaspoon salt

2 eggs

¼ cup catchup

Few drops Tabasco

Coffee Glaze *

Combine all ingredients and shape into loaf. Bake, uncovered, in moderate oven (325° F), 2 hours. During last hour, baste four times with Coffee Glaze. *Makes 6 to 8 servings.*

COFFEE GLAZE*

1 cup firmly packed brown
sugar
1 cup strong coffee
1 teaspoon dry mustard

1 tablespoon mixed
pickling spices, tied in
cheesecloth
1 teaspoon vinegar

Combine all ingredients and bring to boil. Simmer until mixture forms a thick syrup. Remove spice bag.

CREAMED HAM AND EGGS

½ cup (1 stick) butter
or margarine
½ cup flour
1 teaspoon salt
1 teaspoon sugar
2 tablespoons prepared
mustard
¼ cup strong coffee

Few drops Tabasco
1 quart milk or half and
half
1 dozen hard-cooked eggs,
sliced
2 pounds cooked ham, cut
½ inch thick, cubed

Melt butter or margarine. Blend in next 6 ingredients. Add milk; cook and stir over medium heat until smooth and thickened. Add sliced eggs and cubed ham. Heat to serving temperature. *Makes 8 servings.*

THREE-DECKER HAMBURGERS

2 pounds lean beef,
ground
Salt and pepper
½ pound blue cheese
¼ cup minced onion

½ teaspoon Worcestershire
sauce
Few drops Tabasco
Strong, cold coffee

Season beef with salt and pepper. Form into 12 thin patties.
Break up cheese; add onion, Worcestershire sauce, and
Tabasco. Beat until well blended. Add enough coffee to make
soft, spreading consistency. Spread between hamburger
patties, sandwich fashion. Broil to desired degree of doneness,
turning once. Serve on hot, toasted hamburger buns. *Makes
6 servings.*

Cakes, Pies, and Breads

BRAN COFFEECAKE

¼ cup butter or
margarine, melted
½ cup brown sugar, firmly
packed
1½ cups bran flakes

1 teaspoon instant coffee
2 cups prepared biscuit
mix
1 egg, slightly beaten
¾ cup milk

Combine butter or margarine, brown sugar, bran flakes, and coffee. Combine biscuit mix, egg, and milk. Beat hard 30 seconds. Spread half of batter in greased 8-inch-square cake pan. Sprinkle half of cereal mixture over top. Cover with remaining batter and top with remaining cereal. Bake at 375° F for 20 to 25 minutes. Serve warm. *Makes one 8-inch cake.*

BRAZIL-NUT SPICE CAKE

½ cup shortening
1 cup sugar
2 well-beaten eggs
⅔ cup finely chopped
Brazil nuts
1½ cups sifted cake flour
2½ teaspoons baking
powder

½ teaspoon salt
½ teaspoon cinnamon
¼ teaspoon cloves
¼ teaspoon ginger
½ cup strong coffee

Cream shortening, add sugar gradually and cream well. Add well-beaten eggs and beat together until light and fluffy. Stir in the chopped Brazil nuts. Sift together flour, baking powder, salt, and spices. Add these sifted dry ingredients to cake mixture alternately with coffee. Bake in two 8-inch layer-cake pans (greased and lined with waxed paper) in moderate oven (350° F) about 35 minutes. Cool and frost as desired, decorating top of cake with sliced Brazil nuts. *Makes one 8-inch layer cake.*

BUCHE DE NOEL

4 eggs
½ teaspoon salt
¾ cup sugar
2 tablespoons unsweetened
  cocoa
1 teaspoon vanilla

¾ cup pancake mix
1 cup whipping cream
½ cup fine granulated
  sugar
Mocha-Butter Cream*

Grease bottom and sides of 10×15×1-inch jellyroll pan. Line with waxed paper. Grease again thoroughly. Break eggs into bowl; add salt. Beat until thick and lemon-colored. Combine sugar and cocoa. Add gradually to eggs, beating well after each addition. Stir in vanilla and pancake mix. Beat until smooth (batter is quite thin). Spread evenly in pan. Bake at 400° F for 12 minutes. Sprinkle a towel generously with confectioners' sugar. Loosen edges of cake and turn out on towel. Peel off waxed paper and roll cake up in towel. Let stand 20 minutes. Meanwhile, whip cream with fine sugar. Unroll cake. Spread thinly with some of Mocha-Butter Cream, then with whipped cream. Roll up, wrap firmly in aluminum foil and chill (or freeze until ready to use). Frost with remaining Mocha-Butter Cream. Mark with tip of knife or small spatula to resemble bark. Cut off a thin slice. Unroll slice, cut in half and reroll halves to make two small "stumps." Place on top of roll. Decorate with vine and leaves made with green icing. Sprinkle here and there with flaked coconut to resemble snow. *Makes 12 servings.*

MOCHA-BUTTER CREAM*

¾ *pound unsalted butter*
¾ *cup sugar*
1½ *tablespoons unsweetened cocoa*

1½ *tablespoons instant coffee*

Cream butter to soft consistency. Combine sugar, cocoa, and instant coffee. Sift through fine sieve. Add tablespoon at a time to butter, continuing to cream.

BUTTER-BALL COFFEECAKE

3 *cups sifted enriched flour*
¾ *tablespoon salt*
¼ *teaspoon mace*
¼ *cup sugar*
1 *small egg, well beaten*
½ *cup evaporated milk*
⅓ *cup lukewarm water*
2 *tablespoons melted butter*

2 *packages dry active yeast*
⅓ *cup warm (not hot) water*
2 *tablespoons melted butter*
½ *cup mixed sugar and instant coffee*
½ *cup chopped walnuts*
¼ *cup golden seedless raisins*

Combine first 4 ingredients. Combine next 4 ingredients. Dissolve yeast in warm water, add to egg mixture and mix well. Stir in dry ingredients and mix well. Knead on lightly floured board until smooth; place in well-greased bowl, turning once to bring greased side up. Cover; let rise in warm place until double in bulk (about 1 hour). Punch down, cut dough into small pieces, and roll into 40 walnut-size balls. Roll each ball in melted butter, then in coffee sugar. Place one layer of 20 balls in well-greased, 8-inch springform pan, so balls barely touch, leaving a small space in the middle. Sprinkle with half the walnuts and raisins. Make top layer of remaining balls and sprinkle with rest of walnuts and raisins. Pour on remaining butter and instant coffee sugar. Let rise about 45 minutes or until not quite doubled in bulk. Bake at 325° F for 40 to 45 minutes. *Makes 8 to 10 servings.*

BUTTERSCOTCH ICE-CREAM CAKE

1 *package instant*   2 *quarts coffee ice cream*
  butterscotch cake mix   *Butterscotch Sauce**
1 *cup water*   1 *cup toasted, slivered*
2 *eggs, unbeaten*   *almonds*

Empty cake mix into bowl. Add water and eggs (or follow exact directions on package). Beat 3 minutes until smooth and creamy. Pour batter into 2 paper-lined, 9-inch-round layer-cake pans. Bake in moderate oven (350° F), 25 to 30 minutes. Cool. Fill 2 matching pans with ice cream. Place in freezing compartment until very firm. Loosen around edges with spatula or knife. Invert over cake layers and place a warm, moist cloth on pan until ice cream slips out. Return to freezing compartment until ready to serve. Top with Butterscotch Sauce and almonds. *Makes 16 servings.*

CHOCOLATE CAKE A LA CREME

3 squares (1 ounce each) unsweetened chocolate
2½ cups sifted cake flour
1 teaspoon salt
1 teaspoon baking soda
¾ cup shortening
1½ cups sugar
4 eggs
1 cup milk
Mocha-Butter Filling*
2 cups heavy cream, whipped

Melt chocolate, cool slightly. Combine and sift flour, salt, and baking soda. Cream shortening and sugar; beat in eggs until light and fluffy. Add flour mixture alternately with milk, beating well. Stir in chocolate, pour into 2 greased 9-inch layer-cake pans. Bake at 350° F for 30 to 40 minutes. Cool. Fill with Mocha-Butter Filling, frost top and sides with whipped cream. *Makes one 9-inch cake.*

MOCHA-BUTTER FILLING*

1 cup butter or margarine
¾ cup sifted confectioners' sugar
¼ cup instant coffee
¼ cup cocoa
1 teaspoon vanilla extract

Cream butter or margarine; gradually beat in remaining ingredients until fluffy. *Makes Filling for one 9-inch cake.*

CHOCOLATE-CHIP CAKE

1 package white cake mix
2 squares (1 ounce each) unsweetened chocolate, grated
Creamy Coffee Frosting*

Prepare cake according to directions on package. Before pouring batter into pans, stir in grated chocolate. Pour into 2 greased 8-inch layer-cake pans. Bake according to directions on package. Cool layers. Frost with Creamy Coffee Frosting. *Makes two 8-inch layers.*

CREAMY COFFEE FROSTING*

2 3-ounce packages cream cheese
2 tablespoons milk
4 teaspoons instant coffee

4½ cups sifted confectioners' sugar
1 teaspoon pure vanilla extract

Blend cheese and milk and coffee. Add sugar gradually; add vanilla. Beat until smooth. *Makes Frosting for tops and sides of two 8-inch layers.*

CHOCOLATE-CHIP COFFEECAKE

¾ cup milk, scalded
½ cup butter or margarine
⅓ cup sugar
1 teaspoon salt
2 packages yeast
¼ cup lukewarm water

2 eggs, beaten
3½ cups sifted flour
½ cup semisweet chocolate pieces
Coffeecake Topping*

Combine milk, butter or margarine, sugar, and salt. Stir until dissolved. Soften yeast in water; add milk mixture, eggs, and 2½ cups flour. Beat until smooth. Blend in remaining cup of flour and chocolate pieces. Turn dough into well-greased 10-inch angel-cake pan. Sprinkle with topping. Cover; let rise in warm place for 1 hour. Bake at 400° F for 35 to 40 minutes. Turn out of pan immediately. Cool. *Makes one 10-inch coffeecake.*

COFFEECAKE TOPPING*

½ cup flour, sifted
½ cup sugar
¼ cup butter or margarine
½ cup chopped pecans

½ cup semisweet chocolate
pieces
1 teaspoon instant coffee
1 teaspoon vanilla extract

Combine flour and sugar. Cut in butter or margarine until mixture is crumbly. Add remaining ingredients. *Makes topping for one 10-inch coffecake.*

COFFEE BABA AU RHUM

1 package dry active yeast
½ cup warm water
2 cups sifted all-purpose
   flour
½ cup sugar

½ cup butter
½ teaspoon salt
3 eggs, beaten
Coffee Baba-Rum Sauce*

Dissolve yeast in warm water. Add ½ cup of the measured flour and 1 tablespoon of the sugar. Beat smooth. Let rise in warm place until double in bulk. Cream butter; add remaining sugar slowly, creaming until light and fluffy. Add salt and eggs; beat thoroughly. Add remaining flour and yeast mixture. Beat 5 minutes with electric mixer at medium speed or 15 minutes by hand. Pour into a two-quart greased mold. Let rise in warm place until double in bulk. Bake at 350° F for 40 to 50 minutes. Invert on plate. Prick thoroughly with a fork. Pour hot sauce slowly over top so that baba will absorb it. Cool. Serve with whipped cream. *Makes 12 servings.*

COFFEE BABA-RUM SAUCE*

½ cup sweet butter
1 cup confectioners' sugar

½ cup double-strength, hot
   coffee
1 tablespoon brandy

Cream butter and sugar together. Slowly add coffee and brandy, stirring constantly.

COFFEE-SPICE NUT CAKE

2 cups sifted cake flour
½ teaspoon salt
1 teaspoon baking powder
½ teaspoon baking soda
⅛ teaspoon ginger
1 teaspoon cinnamon
½ teaspoon nutmeg

½ teaspoon allspice
1 cup brown sugar
½ cup shortening
¾ cup buttermilk
2 eggs
½ cup chopped pecans
Coffee-Pecan Frosting*

Have all ingredients at room temperature. Sift flour, salt, baking powder, baking soda, and spices together into mixing bowl. Add sugar, shortening, and buttermilk. Beat 200 strokes (or 2 minutes in electric mixer at low speed), scraping the bowl frequently. Add eggs and beat 100 strokes (or 1 minute). Add pecans and beat 100 strokes (or 1 minute). Pour into 2 greased 8-inch cake pans and bake in moderate oven (350° F) for 30 minutes. Remove from pans. When cool, ice with Coffee-Pecan Frosting. *Makes two 8-inch layers.*

COFFEE-PECAN FROSTING*

¼ cup butter
2 cups sifted confectioners'
   sugar
1 egg yolk, beaten

2 tablespoons cold coffee
1½ teaspoons instant
   coffee
½ cup chopped pecans

Cream butter. Gradually add 1 cup of the sugar while beating constantly. Add remaining sugar alternately with egg yolk which has been beaten and blended with cold coffee and instant coffee. Spread on cooled cake. Sprinkle pecans on top of cake. *Makes two 8-inch layers.*

EGGNOG ANGEL CAKE

1 15-ounce package angel-
   food cake mix
1 pint heavy cream
½ cup confectioners' sugar

1 teaspoon instant coffee
½ teaspoon rum extract
2 bananas, thinly sliced
½ cup chopped walnuts

Prepare and bake cake according to directions on package; cool, cut into 3 layers. Combine and whip cream, sugar, coffee, and rum extract. Spread each layer with whipped cream; cover with banana slices. Frost sides and top with remaining cream; sprinkle with chopped nuts. Chill for 3 hours. *Makes one 10-inch cake.*

ICED FRUITCAKE

1½ cups sifted flour
½ teaspoon salt
½ teaspoon baking soda
½ teaspoon cloves
½ teaspoon nutmeg
½ teaspoon cinnamon
1 cup chopped, mixed
    candied fruit

½ cup chopped walnuts
½ cup butter or margarine
½ cup brown sugar,
    firmly packed
2 eggs
½ cup molasses
1 teaspoon lemon extract
Coffee Icing*

Combine and sift dry ingredients. Dredge fruit and nuts with 1 tablespoon flour mixture. Cream butter or margarine. Add sugar gradually, creaming thoroughly. Add eggs, mixing until light and fluffy. Add molasses; blend well. Add fruit and nuts to first mixture; add extract, mix well. Pour into greased, waxed-paper-lined 9×5-inch loaf pan. Bake at 300° F for 1 hour 45 minutes. Cool. Frost with Coffee Icing. *Makes one 9-inch cake.*

COFFEE ICING*

2 tablespoons butter or
    margarine
1½ cups sifted
    confectioners' sugar

1½ teaspoons light cream
2 teaspoons instant coffee
¼ cup chopped walnuts

Cream butter or margarine until light and fluffy. Gradually add sugar; beat until smooth. Add cream and coffee; beat well. Spread on top of Fruitcake, sprinkle with chopped nuts. *Makes Icing for one 9-inch cake.*

Political strategy being discussed in a seventeenth-century English coffeehouse.

MALLOW-WALNUT TORTE

TORTE:

1 cup walnut meats	1 teaspoon baking powder
3 eggs	1/4 teaspoon salt
3/4 cup sugar	1/2 teaspoon cinnamon
1 cup fine zwieback crumbs	

Chop walnuts fine. Beat eggs until light and lemon-colored. Beat in sugar, a little at a time. Combine crumbs, walnuts, baking powder, salt, and cinnamon; fold into egg mixture. Turn into greased 8-inch-square pan. Bake in moderate oven (325° F), 40 to 45 minutes. Cool in pan.

TOPPING:

1½ teaspoons
    (½ envelope) unflavored
    gelatin
¼ cup strong coffee
1 egg, separated
¾ cup milk
1 square (1 ounce)
    unsweetened chocolate,
    finely cut

¼ cup granulated sugar
Few grains salt
6 marshmallows, cut in
    eighths
½ cup whipped cream
1 cup chopped walnut
    meats

Sprinkle gelatin on coffee to soften. Beat egg yolk lightly. Combine milk, egg yolk, chocolate, sugar, and salt. Stir over hot water until mixture thickens slightly. Blend in softened gelatin. Stir until dissolved. Cool until mixture thickens. Fold in marshmallows, stiffly beaten egg white, whipped cream, and walnuts. Spoon over cooled torte and chill until firm. Cut in squares to serve. *Makes 9 servings.*

MOCHA CHOC-A-BLOC

½ pound sweet cooking
    chocolate
½ cup strong coffee

2 egg yolks, slightly beaten
½ teaspoon vanilla
12 ladyfingers

Melt chocolate over hot water. Add coffee and stir until smooth. Pour a little chocolate mixture on egg yolks, add vanilla, and blend. Return to remaining chocolate mixture.

Cook over hot water, stirring constantly, until slightly thickened. Cool to room temperature. Split ladyfingers. Place 3 halves close together and spread with chocolate mixture. Top with 3 ladyfinger halves placed crosswise to first layer and spread with chocolate mixture. Repeat until ladyfingers are all used. Spread remaining chocolate mixture on sides. Chill. Cut in 4 to 6 slices and top with coffee ice cream. *Makes 4 to 6 servings.*

MOCHA RAISIN CAKE

2 cups strong coffee
1 cup sugar
2 tablespoons breakfast cocoa
1 cup seedless raisins, cut up
½ cup shortening
1 cup sugar
½ teaspoon vanilla

2 eggs, unbeaten
2 cups sifted all-purpose flour
½ teaspoon baking soda
2 teaspoons baking powder
½ teaspoon salt
1 teaspoon each cinnamon and nutmeg
½ teaspoon cloves

Combine coffee, sugar, cocoa, and raisins in saucepan. Bring to boil and simmer 10 to 15 minutes. Cool. Cream shortening and add sugar gradually, creaming until light and fluffy. Add vanilla. Add eggs one at a time, beating well after each addition. Mix and sift remaining ingredients. Add, alternating with coffee mixture, and stir thoroughly. Bake in greased, floured 10×10×2-inch pan in moderate oven (350° F) about 1 hour. When cool, place lace paper doily on top. Sift confectioners' sugar on doily; lift off carefully. Cut in squares to serve. *Makes one 10-inch cake.*

NO-BAKE MOCHA CHEESECAKE

½ cup graham-cracker
crumbs
1 tablespoon sugar
1 tablespoon melted butter
1 package (4 ounces)
chocolate pudding or pie-
filling mix
2 envelopes unflavored
gelatin
2 cups strong coffee
½ cup sugar

2 egg yolks, slightly beaten
1 cup creamed cottage
cheese
½ cup instant nonfat dry
milk crystals
½ cup ice water
2 tablespoons lemon juice
½ cup sugar
2 egg whites, stiffly beaten
Chocolate curls

Line bottom of 9×5×3-inch loaf pan with waxed paper or
foil. Mix crumbs with 1 tablespoon sugar and butter. Press
into bottom of pan. Combine pudding mix, gelatin, coffee, ½
cup sugar, and egg yolks in saucepan. Cook over low heat,
stirring constantly, until thickened. Cool thoroughly. Beat
cottage cheese with pudding mixture until blended. Combine
instant crystals with ice water and whip until soft peaks
form (3 to 4 minutes). Add lemon juice and continue whipping until stiff peaks form (3 to 4 minutes longer). Gradually
beat in ½ cup sugar. Fold whipped instant crystals and
egg whites into pudding mixture. Pour into pan over crumb
mixture. Chill until set (about 3 hours). Unmold. Garnish
with chocolate curls. *Makes 8 to 10 servings.*

PLANTER'S CAKE

¾ pound butter
3¾ cups sifted
confectioners' sugar
9 eggs, separated

½ cup strong coffee
1 large spongecake
½ cup rum

Cream butter until soft; add 3 cups of the sugar gradually, continuing to cream until light and fluffy. Add egg yolks, one at a time; beat well after each addition. Add coffee; beat; set aside. Beat egg whites until foamy; slowly add remaining ¾ cup sugar; beat until stiff. Fold egg whites into butter mixture. Slice spongecake into four thin layers. Sprinkle layers of cake with rum. Put layers together with the frosting between and on top. Chill at least 2 hours before serving. *Makes 10 to 12 servings.*

SIX-LAYER COFFEE-CREAM CAKE

2 *eggs*	1 *tablespoon butter*
¼ *teaspoon salt*	1 *cup sifted flour*
1 *cup sugar*	1 *teaspoon baking powder*
1 *teaspoon vanilla*	*Coffee Syrup**
½ *cup milk*	1 *pint whipping cream*

Beat eggs until light. Add salt, sugar, vanilla. Heat milk and butter to boiling; beat in. Mix and sift flour and baking powder; beat in. Divide batter equally among 3 greased, floured, 8-inch layer-cake pans. Bake in moderate oven (350° F), 25 minutes or until done. Cool. Split layers crosswise. Spread cut side of 5 layers and uncut surface on one layer with warm Coffee Syrup. Put layers together with unsweetened whipped cream, glaze top layer. Spread sides with whipped cream. Chill several hours. *Makes 10 to 12 servings.*

COFFEE SYRUP*

Stir 1 cup sugar and ⅔ cup strong coffee over low heat until sugar dissolves. Bring to boiling point. Remove from heat. Stir in 1 tablespoon rum flavoring.

SPICED CHOCOLATE CAKE

1 teaspoon soda
¼ teaspoon salt
½ teaspoon ground
cinnamon
¼ teaspoon ground cloves
2 teaspoons pure vanilla
extract
½ cup (1 stick) butter or
margarine

1¼ cups sugar
3 squares (1 ounce each)
unsweetened chocolate
3 eggs, unbeaten
1½ cups sifted all-purpose
flour
⅔ cup sour milk
Cinnamon-Coffee Frosting*

Add soda, salt, spices, and pure vanilla extract to butter or margarine. Mix well. Gradually blend in sugar. Melt chocolate over hot water and stir into the mixture. Beat in eggs, one at a time. Add flour alternately with sour milk, mixing well after each addition. Beat batter ½ minute. Bake in a well-greased, lightly floured 8×8×2-inch pan in a preheated moderate oven (325° F), 55 minutes or until a cake tester inserted in the center comes out clean. Cool in pan 10 minutes. Turn out onto a wire rack to finish cooling. Frost with Cinnamon-Coffee Frosting. *Makes one 8-inch cake.*

CINNAMON-COFFEE FROSTING*

⅓ cup butter or margarine
3½ cups sifted
confectioners' sugar
3 tablespoons milk or light
cream
1 teaspoon instant coffee

¼ teaspoon ground
cinnamon
1½ teaspoons pure vanilla
extract
1 tablespoon maple-flavored
syrup

Brown butter or margarine in a saucepan large enough for mixing frosting. Add confectioners' sugar alternately with milk or light cream. Stir in coffee, cinnamon, pure vanilla extract, maple-flavored syrup. Spread over top and sides of an 8×8×2-inch cake.

TOFFEE-NUT SUPREME

2 (3⅜-ounce) packages butterscotch pudding mix
2½ cups milk
1 cup heavy cream

2 tablespoons instant coffee
1 cup chopped pecans
4 9-inch pound-cake layers, ¾ inch thick

Combine pudding mix with milk; bring slowly to boiling point, stirring constantly. Remove from heat; cool. Combine cream and coffee; whip to soft peaks. Fold into pudding. Beat ½ minute. Divide mixture in half; add ¾ cup pecans to one half; spread between cake layers. Frost top and sides with remaining pudding mixture. Sprinkle top with remaining ¼ cup pecans. Chill 1½ hours. *Makes one 9-inch cake.*

VELVET SPICE CAKE

2½ cups sifted cake flour
2½ teaspoons baking powder
¼ teaspoon salt
¾ teaspoon cinnamon
¼ teaspoon cloves
½ teaspoon mace

½ cup butter or margarine
1 cup sugar
2 eggs, unbeaten
⅓ cup molasses
¾ cup milk
Pecan-Mocha Frosting*

Sift flour with baking powder, salt, and spices four times. Cream butter or margarine thoroughly; add sugar gradually, and cream until light and fluffy. Add eggs, one at a time, and beat thoroughly after each addition. Add molasses and blend. Add flour mixture, alternately with milk, a small amount at a time. Beat well after each addition. Pour batter into 2 greased 9-inch pans and bake in a quick moderate oven (375° F), 25 to 30 minutes.

PECAN-MOCHA FROSTING*

⅓ cup butter or margarine
4 cups (1 pound) sifted
   confectioners' sugar
4 tablespoons cocoa

¼ teaspoon salt
⅓ cup strong coffee
1½ teaspoons vanilla
1 cup pecans, broken

Cream butter or margarine. Sift sugar, cocoa, and salt together. Add half of this mixture to butter or margarine; blend well. Add remaining sugar mixture alternately with coffee until right consistency to spread. Add vanilla. Spread on top and sides of cooled layers of Velvet Spice Cake. Sprinkle pecans on top and sides of cake. *Makes one 9-inch cake.*

The façade of Caffè Caselli appears today much as it did early in the nineteenth century, when it was favored by Florence's wealthy merchants.

WALNUT CAKE

4 eggs, separated	½ cup finely chopped
½ cup sugar	walnuts
1 tablespoon grated orange	Mocha Frosting*
rind	

Beat yolks with ¼ cup sugar until thick and lemon-colored. Mix in rind. Beat egg whites until stiff but not dry. Gradually add remaining ¼ cup sugar. Continue beating until mixture is stiff and glossy. Fold whites and nuts alternately into yolk mixture. Pour batter into ungreased 9-inch springform pan. Bake at 375° F for 45 minutes. Cool. Frost with Mocha Frosting. *Makes one 9-inch cake.*

MOCHA FROSTING*

1 square (1 ounce)	¼ cup heavy cream
unsweetened chocolate	⅛ teaspoon salt
1½ tablespoons butter or	2 teaspoons instant coffee
margarine	1 cup confectioners' sugar

Melt chocolate. Stir in butter or margarine and cream. Heat slightly. Add salt to chocolate mixture; blend well. Remove from heat; cool. Add coffee. Beat in sugar gradually until smooth. *Makes Frosting for top and sides of one 9-inch cake.*

ALMOND-CREAM PIE

1 package vanilla pudding	1 teaspoon almond extract
mix	Coffee Coconut Shell*
½ cup chopped, toasted	
almonds	

Prepare pudding mix as directed on package; stir in almonds; add almond extract. Cool slightly, stirring once or twice. Pour into Coffee Coconut Shell. Chill.

COFFEE COCONUT SHELL*

1 can (3½ ounces) coconut, flaked
1 cup strong, hot coffee
2 tablespoons butter or margarine

Empty can of coconut into bowl. Add the strong, hot coffee. Let stand 30 to 40 minutes, then drain. Pat dry between layers of absorbent paper. Rub butter or margarine on bottom and sides of 9-inch piepan and press coconut on butter. Bake in moderate oven (350° F) 10 minutes. Cool. *Makes one 9-inch pie shell.*

COFFEE BAVARIAN PIE

1 envelope unflavored
    gelatin
6 tablespoons sugar, divided
⅛ teaspoon salt
1 tablespoon instant coffee

2 eggs, separated
1¼ cups milk
1 (9-inch) baked pie shell
1 cup heavy cream, whipped

Mix gelatin, 2 tablespoons of the sugar, salt, and instant coffee in top of double boiler. Beat together egg yolks and milk; add to gelatin mixture. Cook over boiling water, stirring constantly until gelatin dissolves and mixture thickens slightly, about 6 minutes. Chill until mixture is slightly thicker than the consistency of unbeaten egg white. Beat egg whites until stiff, but not dry. Gradually add remaining 4 tablespoons sugar and beat until very stiff. Fold into gelatin mixture. Fold in whipped cream. Turn into pie shell; chill until firm. If desired, garnish with additional sweetened whipped cream and banana slices, and sprinkle with instant coffee. *Makes one 9-inch pie.*

COFFEE AND CORNFLAKES PIE

1 tablespoon gelatin
¼ cup cold coffee
2 egg yolks
⅔ cup sweetened,
  condensed milk
¼ teaspoon salt

1½ cups strong, hot coffee
2 egg whites, stiffly beaten
1 tablespoon margarine
1 cup cornflakes, rolled
1 tablespoon sugar or honey

Soften gelatin with cold coffee. Beat egg yolks slightly; add condensed milk and salt. Dissolve gelatin with hot coffee and stir gradually into egg-milk mixture. Place in refrigerator until mixture begins to set and fold into stiffly beaten egg whites. Pour into a deep piepan or shallow serving dish with straight sides. Melt margarine, stir in rolled cornflakes and sugar or honey. Sprinkle over top and return to refrigerator until ready to serve. To serve, cut into pie-shaped pieces and lift carefully with pie server. *Makes 4 servings.*

COFFEE-COCONUT PRUNE PIE

1 cup chopped, plumped
  prunes
⅓ cup prune juice
2 tablespoons grated orange
  rind
3 eggs
½ cup light-brown sugar
¼ cup granulated sugar
½ teaspoon salt

1 envelope unflavored
  gelatin
1 cup sour cream
1 (9-inch) Coffee Coconut
  Shell*
½ cup heavy cream,
  whipped
6 plumped prune halves
Maraschino cherries

Place chopped prunes, prune juice, and orange rind in saucepan. Beat eggs; add sugars, salt, gelatin, and sour cream; add to prunes. Cook over medium heat about 10 minutes, stirring constantly, until thickened. Cool slightly. Pour into Coffee Coconut Shell. Chill until firm. Just before serving, garnish with whipped cream, prune halves, and cherries. *Makes 6 servings.*

COFFEE COCONUT SHELL *

Combine one 3½-ounce can flaked coconut and 1 cup very strong coffee; let stand 30 to 40 minutes. Drain and spread coconut on paper toweling; pat to absorb excess liquid. Spread 9-inch pie plate with 2 tablespoons softened butter; sprinkle in coconut and pat against bottom and sides of plate. Bake at 350° F for 10 minutes. *Makes one 9-inch pie shell.*

COFFEE-SUNDAE PIE

18 cream-filled chocolate cookies	1 tablespoon butter or margarine
⅓ cup melted butter or margarine	1 small can (⅔ cup) evaporated milk
2 squares (1 ounce each) unsweetened chocolate	1 quart coffee ice cream
½ cup sugar	1 cup whipping cream
	½ cup chopped walnuts

Crush cookies to fine crumbs with rolling pin and add melted butter or margarine. Mix well. Press around sides and on bottom of 9-inch piepan. Chill. Melt chocolate over hot water and stir in sugar and 1 tablespoon butter or margarine. Add evaporated milk slowly. Cook over hot water, stirring occasionally, until thickened. Chill. Fill pie shell with ice cream and spread chocolate mixture over the top. Whip cream and spoon over surface of pie. Sprinkle with walnuts. Serve at once or store in freezer or freezing compartment of refrigerator until ready to serve. *Makes 6 servings.*

COFFEE-WALNUT PARFAIT PIE

1¼ cups strong coffee
1 package orange-flavored
gelatin

1 pint coffee ice cream
1 cup broken walnuts
1 (9-inch) baked pie shell

Heat coffee until very hot, but not boiling. Add gelatin and stir until dissolved. Cut ice cream in eight pieces, add at once and stir until dissolved. Chill in refrigerator a few minutes until mixture "mounds" when dropped from a spoon. Fold in walnuts; spoon into pie shell. Chill until firm. Garnish top with whipped cream and whole walnuts if desired. *Makes 6 servings.*

CREAMY COFFEE-CHIFFON PIE

1 envelope unflavored
gelatin
1 cup strong coffee, divided
1 cup sugar, divided
½ teaspoon salt
¾ cup strong, hot coffee

1 cup heavy cream, divided
3 eggs, separated
1 teaspoon vanilla
¼ teaspoon cream of tartar
1 (9-inch) baked pie shell
Flaked coconut

Soften gelatin in ¼ cup cold coffee. Combine ½ cup sugar, salt, remaining coffee, and ½ cup cream in saucepan. Stir over low heat until scalding point is reached. Beat egg yolks and add hot mixture slowly. Return to saucepan and stir over low heat until boiling point is reached. Stir in softened gelatin. Chill until partially set, then beat until smooth. Add vanilla. Whip remaining cream and fold in. Beat egg whites until they form soft peaks. Add cream of tartar. Add remaining sugar slowly, beating well after each addition. Fold coffee mixture carefully into this meringue. Spoon into pie shell. Garnish with toasted, flaked coconut. *Makes one 9-inch pie.*

INSTANT-COFFEE-EGGNOG CHIFFON PIE

1 *envelope unflavored*
  gelatin
2 *tablepoons sugar*
2¼ *cups bottled*
  nonalcoholic eggnog

2 *teaspoons instant coffee*
½ *cup heavy cream,*
  whipped
1 *(8-inch) baked pie shell*

Combine gelatin and sugar in top of double boiler. Stir in 1 cup of the cold eggnog. Place over boiling water and stir until gelatin and sugar are dissolved. Remove from heat; stir in instant coffee and remaining eggnog. Chill until slightly thicker than the consistency of unbeaten egg white. Fold in whipped cream. Turn into baked pie shell; chill until firm. Garnish with additional whipped cream, shaved chocolate, chopped maraschino cherries, orange peel, and citron. *Makes one 8-inch pie.*

LAYERED MOCHA PIE

1 *(8-inch) unbaked pie shell*
½ *cup double-strength*
  coffee
½ *cup evaporated milk*
1½ *cups sugar, divided*

¼ *teaspoon salt*
½ *teaspoon rum flavoring*
4 *eggs, separated*
2 *squares (1 ounce each)*
  unsweetened chocolate

Line 8-inch pie pan with pastry. Combine coffee, evaporated milk, 1 cup sugar, and salt; heat until warm. Add rum flavoring. Beat egg yolks; add coffee mixture slowly. Grate chocolate; add; pour into pie shell. Bake in oven (425° F), 10 minutes. Reduce heat to 375°; bake 35 minutes longer. Beat egg whites stiff; add remaining ½ cup sugar while beating. Swirl on pie; return to oven; bake at 325° for 20 minutes. *Makes one 8-inch pie.*

MOCHA CHIFFON PIE I

1 *envelope unflavored*
   gelatin
½ *cup sugar, divided*
¼ *teaspoon salt*
½ *cup evaporated milk*
½ *cup water*
2 *eggs, separated*
1 *6-ounce package (1 cup)*
   semisweet chocolate
   morsels

1 *teaspoon vanilla*
⅔ *cup ice-cold evaporated*
   milk, whipped
1 *(9-inch) baked pie shell*
½ *cup heavy cream,*
   whipped

Combine gelatin, ¼ cup of the sugar, and salt in top of double boiler. Stir in the ½ cup evaporated milk and water; add egg yolks and mix well. Add chocolate morsels. Cook over boiling water until chocolate is melted, stirring often. Remove from heat and beat with rotary beater until smooth. Add vanilla. Chill until the mixture mounds slightly when dropped from a spoon. Beat egg whites until stiff, but not dry; gradually beat in remaining ¼ cup sugar. Fold beaten egg whites and whipped evaporated milk into gelatin mixture. Turn into baked pie shell and chill until firm. Garnish with whipped cream. *Makes one 9-inch pie.*

Note: to whip evaporated milk, chill milk in freezer tray of refrigerator until soft ice crystals form around edge, about 10 minutes. Turn into chilled bowl and whip with rotary beater on high speed of electric mixer until milk is stiff.

MOCHA CHIFFON PIE II

1 envelope unflavored
gelatin
1 tablespoon instant coffee
½ cup sugar, divided
⅛ teaspoon salt

2 eggs, separated
1¾ cups bottled chocolate
milk, divided
1 cup heavy cream, whipped
1 (9-inch) baked pie shell

Mix together gelatin, instant coffee, ¼ cup of the sugar, and salt in top of double boiler. Beat together egg yolks and 1 cup of the chocolate milk; stir into gelatin mixture. Cook over boiling water, stirring until gelatin dissolves and mixture thickens slightly (about 6 minutes). Remove from heat; stir in remaining ¾ cup chocolate milk. Chill until mixture is the consistency of unbeaten egg white. Beat egg whites until stiff, but not dry. Gradually add remaining ¼ cup sugar and beat until very stiff. Fold in gelatin mixture; fold in whipped cream. Turn into pie shell; chill until firm. *Makes one 9-inch pie.*

MOCHA-PECAN CHIFFON PIE

1 envelope unflavored
gelatin
¼ cup cold water
3 tablespoons cocoa
1 cup sugar, divided
¾ cup water
2 teaspoons instant
coffee
3 eggs, separated

1 teaspoon vanilla extract
½ teaspoon imitation rum
extract
¼ teaspoon salt
¾ cup finely chopped
pecans
1 (9-inch) baked pie shell
Pecan halves
Whipping cream

Soften gelatin in cold water. Combine in heavy saucepan the cocoa, ¾ cup sugar, water, and instant coffee; stir to dissolve sugar. Bring to boil, and let cook gently for 4 to 5 minutes, stirring constantly. Beat egg yolks slightly. Pour hot mixture on top slowly, stirring constantly. Return to saucepan. Stir over heat until mixture thickens. Remove from heat. Add gelatin, vanilla and rum extracts; stir until gelatin dissolves. Chill until mixture mounds slightly when dropped from a spoon. Beat egg whites and salt until foamy. Beat in remaining ¼ cup sugar by single teaspoonfuls, beating constantly; beat until whites stand in stiff peaks. Fold with pecans into gelatin mixture. Turn into baked pie shell. Chill until set. Garnish with pecan halves and whipped cream. *Makes one 9-inch pie.*

THANKSGIVING COFFEE-EGGNOG PIE

2 envelopes unflavored gelatin	1 teaspoon brandy flavoring
½ cup cold coffee	1 cup heavy cream
2 cups hot coffee	⅛ teaspoon salt
½ cup sugar	1 (9-inch) baked pie shell
2 eggs, separated	1 square (1 ounce) unsweetened chocolate

Soften gelatin in cold coffee; dissolve in hot coffee. Add sugar; stir until dissolved. Pour slowly on well-beaten egg yolks. Chill until consistency of unbeaten egg whites. Add brandy flavoring. Whip cream; fold in. Beat egg whites with salt; fold in. Spoon into pie shell. Chill until set. Garnish with shaved chocolate. *Makes one 9-inch pie.*

UPSIDE-DOWN
COFFEE CHIFFON PIE

1 envelope unflavored
   gelatin
¾ cup cold water
½ cup sugar
¼ teaspoon salt
3 teaspoons instant coffee
¼ teaspoon vanilla
½ cup nonfat dry milk

½ cup water
½ cup chocolate-cookie
   crumbs
1 tablespoon butter or
   margarine, melted
1 cup shredded coconut,
   chopped

Soften gelatin in top of double boiler in cold water; dissolve
over boiling water. Mix together sugar, salt, and instant coffee; add to gelatin mixture and stir until dissolved. Add vanilla. Chill mixture until slightly thicker than the consistency
of unbeaten egg white; beat until light and fluffy. Sprinkle
nonfat dry milk over water; beat with rotary beater or electric
mixer on high speed for 10 minutes; fold in gelatin mixture.
Turn into a 10-inch pie plate; chill until firm. Combine
cookie crumbs and butter; toss lightly. To serve, loosen filling
from sides of plate with tip of paring knife; cut into 8 wedges.
Top alternate wedges with crumbs; sprinkle remaining wedges
with coconut. *Makes 8 servings.*

WEST INDIES FRUIT PIE

1 cup cubed fresh (or
   frozen) pineapple
2 fresh pears, peeled,
   quartered, cored, diced
2 bananas, diced
1 cup dried figs, finely diced
½ cup light-brown sugar,
   firmly packed

¼ teaspoon salt
1 tablespoon flour
Grated rind of one lemon
Juice of one lemon
1 (9-inch) unbaked pie shell
1 (9-inch) unbaked pie top
Coffee Sauce*

Combine pineapple, pears, bananas, figs. Add brown sugar, salt, flour, grated lemon rind, lemon juice; mix well. Pour into pie shell; cover with pastry top; crimp edges. Bake 15 minutes at 425° F; reduce heat to 350°; continue baking 45 minutes longer. Serve hot with Coffee Sauce. *Makes 6 servings.*

A characteristic Dutch coffeehouse of about 1650 (from a sketch by J. Beauvarlet, one of the first to use the coffee-house as a subject in art).

COFFEE SAUCE*

2 tablespoons sugar
2 teaspoons cornstarch
¼ teaspoon cinnamon

2 tablespoons water
½ cup strong coffee

Combine sugar, cornstarch, cinnamon. Add water, coffee; mix well. Cook until sauce thickens, stirring constantly. Serve hot over pie.

BREAD IN A CASSEROLE

2 cups sifted flour
1 teaspoon baking soda
1½ teaspoons salt
1 teaspoon instant coffee
½ cup butter or margarine, melted

⅔ cup sugar
2 eggs
1⅓ cups (approximately 3) mashed bananas

Combine and sift flour, baking soda, salt, and coffee. Combine butter or margarine, sugar, eggs, and bananas. Beat well. Add dry ingredients, mixing just enough to blend. Pour into greased, oval, 1½-quart casserole. Bake at 350° F for 1 hour. *Makes 1 loaf.*

DATE-APRICOT COFFEE-LOAF BREAD

1 cup honey
½ cup boiling coffee
½ cup dried apricots, sliced
1 cup dates, diced
1 cup walnuts, coarsely chopped
1 egg
¼ cup salad oil

1 cup milk
3 cups all-purpose flour, sifted
3 teaspoons baking powder
1 teaspoon salt
½ teaspoon cinnamon or pure vanilla extract

Combine honey, boiling coffee, apricots, and dates. Allow to stand until cool, add walnuts. In mixing bowl beat egg slightly, add oil and milk. Fold in prepared fruit and sifted dry ingredients. Mix only until dry ingredients are blended. Pour batter into greased, waxed-paper-lined 9×5×3-inch loaf pan. Let stand 15 minutes. Bake at 350° F about 1¼ hours. Cool in pan 5 minutes, remove paper and cool on wire rack. *Makes 1 loaf.*

OATMEAL BREAD

¾ *cup boiling water*	3 *teaspoons salt*
1 *cup hot coffee*	2 *packages granular yeast*
1 *cup rolled oats*	¼ *cup lukewarm water*
⅓ *cup shortening*	2 *eggs, unbeaten*
½ *cup light molasses*	5½ *cups sifted flour*

Combine boiling water, coffee, rolled oats, shortening, molasses, and salt. Cool to lukewarm. Add yeast to lukewarm water; stir until thoroughly dissolved. Add to coffee mixture. Blend in eggs. Add flour gradually, mix until well blended and place in greased bowl. Cover and chill at least two hours or until needed. Shape chilled dough into two loaves; place in two greased 9×4×3-inch loaf pans; cover. Let rise in warm place (80° to 85° F) until doubled in bulk (about 2 hours). Bake in moderate oven (350° F), 1 hour. *Makes 2 loaves.*

Pastries, Cookies, and Confections

COFFEE

Voluptuous berry! Where may mortals find
Nectars divine that can with thee compare,
When, having dined, we sip thy essence rare,
And feel towards wit and repartee inclined?

Thou wert of sneering, cynical Voltaire,
The only friend; thy power urged Balzac's mind
To glorious effort; surely Heaven designed
Thy devotees superior joys to share.
Whene'er I breathe thy fumes, 'mid Summer stars.

The Orient's splendent pomps my vision greet.
Damascus, with its myriad minarets, gleams!
I see thee, smoking, in immense bazaars,
Or yet, in dim seraglios, at the feet
Of blond Sultanas, pale with amorous dreams!

Francis Saltus Saltus
(d. 1889) from "Flasks and Flagons"

ALMOND-MOCHA MERINGUES

1 6-ounce package (1 cup) semisweet chocolate pieces
3 egg whites
1 teaspoon instant coffee

⅛ teaspoon almond extract
1 cup sugar
¼ cup finely chopped blanched almonds

Melt chocolate over low heat. Cool. Combine egg whites, coffee, and almond extract. Beat until stiff but not dry. Add sugar gradually, beating until very stiff. Fold in almonds and chocolate. Drop by teaspoonfuls 2 inches apart on greased baking sheet. Bake at 350° F for 10 to 12 minutes. Remove immediately from pan to prevent sticking. *Makes 4 dozen meringues.*

BAKED COFFEE DOUGHNUTS

2 cups prepared biscuit mix
½ cup plus 2 tablespoons sugar
1 teaspoon instant coffee

½ cup milk
1 egg
¼ cup butter or margarine, melted

Combine biscuit mix, 2 tablespoons sugar, and coffee. Add milk and egg. Mix well. Place on lightly floured board or pastry cloth. Knead 2 or 3 times. Dough will be soft. Roll to ½ inch thickness. Cut with floured doughnut cutter. Save the "holes" to bake. Hold opposite sides of ring with fingers; twist to make figure of eight. Place on baking sheet. Bake at 400° F for 10 to 12 minutes. Remove from oven; immediately dip in butter or margarine; then in remaining sugar, coating all sides. Serve warm. *Makes 10 doughnuts.*

CALIFORNIA FRUIT BARS

3 cups cooked apricots,
    drained
1¾ cups sugar
¼ cup apricot liquor
2 cups sifted flour
1 teaspoon salt

½ teaspoon baking soda
1 teaspoon instant coffee
¾ cup butter or margarine
¾ cup chopped walnuts
Whipped cream

Combine apricots, ¾ cup sugar, and apricot liquor. Cook, stirring constantly, over medium heat until thickened. Cool. Combine and sift flour, salt, baking soda, and coffee. Cream butter or margarine with remaining 1 cup sugar; blend with dry ingredients to form crumbs. Add nuts. Place 3 cups of crumb mixture in bottom and sides of 13×9½-inch baking pan. Add apricot filling. Bake at 400° F for 10 minutes. Sprinkle with remaining crumbs. Bake 20 to 25 minutes longer. Cut into bars and serve warm with whipped cream. *Serves 12.*

COFFEE-MALLOW HEARTS

1 envelope unflavored
    gelatin
¼ cup cold coffee
2 cups miniature
    marshmallows
¼ cup hot coffee

2 packages cake layers
    (2 layers in each)
1 package instant vanilla
    pudding
1 cup heavy cream
½ cup cold coffee

Soften gelatin in cold coffee. Combine marshmallows and hot coffee in saucepan and dissolve over low heat. Add softened gelatin and stir until dissolved. Cool. Split each cake layer through to form two thin layers. Using an individual heart-shaped mold, cut 3 hearts from each thin layer, making

24 cut-outs. Press 1 cut-out in each of 12 lightly oiled individual heart molds. When gelatin mixture is cool, prepare pudding mix, using cream and coffee instead of milk called for in package directions. When pudding has set, fold in gelatin mixture. Fill heart molds to top with this mixture. Press remaining cut-outs on top; chill. Unmold to serve and garnish with whipped cream and candied violets, if desired. *Makes 12.*

COFFEE-PECAN CORNUCOPIAS

1 *package pie-crust mix*	*Few grains salt*
2 *tablespoons sugar*	*½ cup heavy cream*
1 *tablespoon instant coffee*	*½ cup chopped pecans*

Prepare pie-crust mix as directed on package. Roll out thin. Cut eight 4-inch squares. Fold over to form cornucopias, turning narrow end in a curve. Stuff wide opening with paper toweling. Bake in hot oven (425° F), 10 to 12 minutes or until golden brown. Remove toweling and cool on rack. Meanwhile, combine sugar, instant coffee, and salt; dissolve in a little of the cream. Add remaining cream. Chill. Whip until stiff. Fold in about ⅓ cup of the chopped pecans. Fill cornucopias with this mixture. Scatter remaining pecan meats on surface of cream. *Makes 8 cornucopias.*

EGGNOG TARTS

3 *eggs, separated*	*¼ cup water*
¾ cup sugar, divided	*½ teaspoon rum flavoring*
⅛ teaspoon salt	*6 baked tart shells*
¼ teaspoon nutmeg	*Semisweet chocolate pieces*
1 *cup hot milk*	*Long gumdrops*
1 *cup hot coffee*	
1 *envelope unflavored gelatin*	

Beat egg yolks until thick and lemon-colored. Beat in ½ cup sugar, salt, and nutmeg. Combine hot milk and coffee; add slowly to egg-yolk mixture. Cook over hot water, stirring until mixture coats spoon. Remove from heat. Soften gelatin in cold water, dissolve in hot-milk mixture and add rum flavoring. Cool until slightly thickened. Beat egg whites until stiff but not dry. Beat in remaining ¼ cup sugar slowly. Fold in egg-yolk mixture. Spoon into tart shells, keeping top surface as smooth as possible. Chill until set. Make clock faces with chocolate pieces and slivers of gumdrops. *Makes 6 tarts.*

PECAN PETAL TARTS

2 packages pie-crust mix
1 egg
¾ cup brown sugar
2 teaspoons instant coffee
Few grains salt

1 tablespoon melted butter
 or margarine
½ teaspoon vanilla
⅔ cup coarsely broken
 pecans

Prepare pie crust as directed on package, and divide in half. Roll out each half ⅛ inch thick. Cut pastry into 72 2-inch circles. Place one circle in bottom of each of 12 muffin cups. Arrange 5 overlapping circles around inside of each muffin cup, pressing securely. Beat egg just enough to blend yolk and white. Combine sugar, instant coffee, and salt; add gradually to egg, beating well after each addition. Add melted butter and vanilla. Sprinkle pecans evenly into muffin cups. Spoon filling over pecans, filling cups not quite to top. Bake in moderate oven (350° F), 20 minutes or until set. Garnish with whipped cream. *Makes 1 dozen.*

SPANISH COFFEE-MERINGUE TART

MERINGUE SHELL:

4 egg whites, at room
temperature
¼ teaspoon cream of tartar

¼ teaspoon salt
1 tablespoon instant coffee
1 cup granulated sugar

Combine egg whites, cream of tartar, and salt. With electric mixer or rotary beater, beat egg whites until stiff, but not dry. Gradually add sugar, 1 tablespoon at a time, beating well after each addition. Add coffee with last sugar and continue beating until very stiff, glossy peaks form. Spread half of meringue on bottom of well-buttered 10-inch pie plate. Using a spatula or pastry tube, swirl or pipe remaining meringue around sides and rim of plate, making a decorative edge. Bake in a slow oven 1 hour, or until crisp to the touch. Cool before filling.

FRUIT FILLING:

2 bananas, sliced
1 cup whole grapes
2 tablespoons lemon juice
2 oranges, sliced

½ cup whole maraschino
cherries (about 20
cherries)

Combine bananas and grapes with lemon juice. Arrange with orange slices and cherries in meringue shell. Garnish with additional cherries, as desired. Serve with Spanish Cream Sauce.*

SPANISH CREAM SAUCE*

½ cup granulated sugar
½ cup all-purpose flour
2 cups milk
4 egg yolks

2 tablespoons butter or
margarine
2 teaspoons vanilla
1 cup heavy cream, whipped

Combine sugar, flour, milk, egg yolks, and butter or margarine. Cook over hot water, stirring constantly, until thickened. Add vanilla. Cool, stirring occasionally. Fold in whipped cream. Serve with Meringue Tart. *Makes 8 servings.*

TINY COFFEE CREAM PUFFS

½ cup butter or margarine
1 cup boiling water
1 cup flour, sifted
Few grains salt
4 eggs
1 cup heavy cream

⅓ cup very fine granulated
sugar
1 cup confectioners' sugar,
sifted
Coffee Essence*

Combine butter and boiling water in saucepan, and bring to boiling point. Combine flour and salt; add all at once. Mix well. Cook, stirring constantly until mixture forms smooth, compact mass. Remove from heat. Add unbeaten eggs, one at a time, beating vigorously after each addition. Drop by teaspoons on greased baking sheet, at least one inch apart. Bake in hot oven (400° F), 25 minutes or until puffs are golden brown and set. Cool. Make a slit in side of each puff. Whip cream; add fine granulated sugar slowly, while whipping. Fold in 1 tablespoon of Coffee Essence. Fill cream puffs. Add 1 tablespoon Coffee Essence to confectioners' sugar; mix well. If desired, add additional Coffee Essence to make a thin frosting and use to top cream puffs. *Makes about 3 dozen.*

COFFEE ESSENCE*

Combine ½ cup boiling water and 2 tablespoons instant coffee. Stir well and cool.

COFFEE BUTTER BITS

½ cup cornstarch   1 cup flour, sifted
½ cup confectioners' sugar 1 cup butter or margarine
1 tablespoon instant coffee

Mix and sift cornstarch, confectioners' sugar, instant coffee, and flour. Have butter or margarine at room temperature. Blend butter into dry ingredients with a spoon until a soft dough is formed. Chill about 1 hour. Shape into balls about 1 inch in diameter. Place on ungreased cookie sheet about 1½ inches apart. Flatten cookies with lightly floured fork. Bake in slow oven (300° F), 20 to 25 minutes. *Makes about 3 dozen cookies.*

COFFEE-NUT COOKIES

2 cups sifted flour   2 eggs, well beaten
1 teaspoon baking soda   ¼ cup milk
1 cup butter or margarine   1 cup walnuts, finely
1 teaspoon salt   chopped
2 teaspoons instant coffee
2 cups brown sugar, firmly
  packed

Combine and sift flour and baking soda. Cream butter or margarine, salt, and coffee. Add sugar gradually; beat until light and fluffy. Add eggs and mix. Add one cup of flour mixture and milk; mix well. Add remaining flour mixture and nuts; mix thoroughly. Force through cookie press onto greased baking sheet. Bake at 375° F for 8 to 10 minutes. *Makes 5 to 6 dozen cookies.*

HUNGARIAN COFFEE CRESCENTS

1 cup sweet butter
1 8-ounce package cream
cheese
¼ teaspoon salt
2 cups flour, sifted

2½ teaspoons instant coffee
½ teaspoon ginger
½ cup sugar
1 cup finely chopped
walnuts

Cream butter, cheese, and salt. Add flour; blend thoroughly. Form into 14 balls. Chill for 2 hours. Roll each ball to 6-inch circle on floured board. Cut into quarters. Combine coffee, ginger, sugar, and nuts. Place rounded teaspoonful on each quarter. Fold pointed edge to wide edge, press to seal; form into crescents. Place one inch apart on ungreased baking sheet. Bake at 350° F for 12 to 15 minutes. *Makes 4½ dozen cookies.*

LEBKUCHEN WITH COFFEE ICING

¾ cup honey
½ cup granulated sugar
¼ cup brown sugar
2 eggs, beaten
2½ cups flour, sifted
1¼ teaspoons cinnamon
¼ teaspoon ground cloves
⅛ teaspoon allspice

½ cup finely chopped
candied citron
½ cup finely chopped
candied lemon peel
¾ cup chopped blanched
almonds
Coffee Icing*

Bring honey to boiling point in large, heavy saucepan. Cool. Blend in sugars. Add eggs and beat well. Sift together flour, cinnamon, cloves, and allspice. Add to egg mixture gradually, beating well after each addition. Stir in fruit and almonds. Spread dough into well-greased 10½×15½-inch jellyroll pan. Bake in moderate oven (350° F), 20 to 25 minutes. When cool, spread with Coffee Icing. Cut diagonally for form cookie diamonds. *Makes about 3 dozen cookies.*

COFFEE ICING*

3 cups confectioners' sugar
1 tablespoon instant coffee
3 tablespoons milk or light cream

Blend confectioners' sugar, coffee, and milk or cream.

MOLASSES COOKIES

4 cups flour, sifted
1 teaspoon baking soda
1 teaspoon salt
2 teaspoons instant coffee
½ teaspoon ginger

½ teaspoon nutmeg
1 cup shortening
2 cups sugar, divided
1 cup molasses
2 eggs

Combine and sift flour, baking soda, salt, coffee, and spices. Cream shortening, 1 cup sugar, and molasses. Add eggs one at a time, beating well after each addition. Add dry ingredients. Mix well. Pinch off a ball of dough about the size of a walnut. Dip in remaining 1 cup sugar; place on greased baking sheet. Bake at 350° F for 12 to 15 minutes. *Makes 5 to 6 dozen cookies.*

NORWEGIAN COFFEE CROWNS

4 hard-cooked egg yolks
1 cup soft butter or
  margarine

½ cup sugar
2 cups flour, sifted
½ teaspoon instant coffee

Force egg yolks through a sieve. Add to butter or margarine, mixing thoroughly. Gradually add sugar; continue creaming until well blended. Add flour and coffee. Beat well. Force dough through cookie press, using crown plate, onto ungreased baking sheet. Bake at 375° F for 10 to 12 minutes. *Makes 5 dozen crowns.*

A typical mid-seventeenth-century German coffeehouse,
popular gathering place for artists and thinkers.

WALNUT-COFFEE SANDIES

6 *tablespoons butter or*
margarine
2½ *tablespoons*
confectioners' sugar
1 *cup sifted cake flour*
1 *teaspoon instant coffee*

1 *teaspoon ice water*
1 *teaspoon vanilla extract*
½ *cup finely chopped*
walnuts
Confectioners' sugar

Cream butter or margarine; add 2½ tablespoons sugar; beat
well. Add flour, coffee, water, vanilla extract and walnuts.
Blend well. Chill for 2 hours. Form into 1-inch balls. Place

1 inch apart on ungreased baking sheet. Bake at 300° F for 30 to 35 minutes. Cool slightly. Roll in confectioners' sugar. *Makes 2 dozen Sandies.*

COBANA BARS

1¾ *cups flour, sifted*
2 *teaspoons baking powder*
½ *teaspoon salt*
2 *tablespoons instant coffee*
½ *cup shortening*

1 *cup sugar*
1 *teaspoon lemon extract*
3 *eggs, well beaten*
1 *cup mashed bananas* (3 *fully ripe bananas*)
½ *cup chopped walnuts*

Mix and sift flour, baking powder, salt, and instant coffee. Cream shortening and sugar. Add lemon extract and eggs. Mix well. Add flour mixture alternately with mashed bananas. Stir in walnuts. Bake in greased 8×12×2-inch pan, in moderate oven (350° F) for ½ hour. Cool in pan and cut into bars 4 inches long and 1 inch wide. Frost with plain confectioners'-sugar icing and sprinkle with chopped walnuts. *Makes 24 bars.*

SUGARLESS CONFECTIONS

½ *pound prunes*
1 *package figs*
1½ *cups raisins*

1½ *cups walnuts or pecans*
½ *teaspoon salt*
¼ *cup cold coffee*

Pit prunes. Combine with other fruit and put through meat grinder. Chop nuts, and add to fruit. Add salt to coffee; stir into mixture. Knead with fingers until well mixed. Dampen hands and form into small balls, cones, and rolls. Decorate balls with small, whole almonds, pecans, or walnuts. *Makes 30 to 40 confections.*

Sauces and Frostings

In addition to the recipes in this chapter, there are many additional recipes for sauces and frostings given throughout with the recipes for which they are specially suited. The reader will be able to locate these toppings by consulting the index.

BITTERSWEET MOCHA FROSTING

1 cup sugar	½ cup strong coffee
1 cup cocoa	½ cup broken nutmeats
¼ teaspoon salt	¼ teaspoon vanilla

Combine sugar, cocoa, and salt in saucepan; blend in coffee. Cook over low heat until smooth and glossy, stirring often (about 15 minutes). Cool. Beat in nutmeats and vanilla. Chill until firm. Spread on cake with spatula dipped in hot water. *Makes enough frosting for 24 tiny cup cakes or top and sides of two 8-inch layers.*

COFFEE MARSHMALLOW SAUCE

½ cup light corn syrup
½ cup sugar
⅓ cup strong, cold coffee
⅛ teaspoon salt

1 egg white
⅛ teaspoon cream of tartar
1 teaspoon vanilla

Combine the syrup, sugar, coffee, and salt. Stir over low heat until sugar dissolves. Cook without stirring to 234° F, or until a little of the syrup forms a soft ball when dipped in cold water. Beat egg white frothy and add cream of tartar. Beat stiff. Pour syrup mixture slowly on egg white, beating constantly. Continue to beat until thick and glossy. Add 1 teaspoon vanilla. *Makes 2 cups.*

COFFEE-SCOTCH FROSTING

¼ cup butter or margarine
½ cup brown sugar

3 cups confectioners' sugar
¼ cup strong, cold coffee

Cream butter or margarine. Add brown sugar and continue creaming until smooth. Add confectioners' sugar and coffee alternately, beating constantly. Use as filling between split layers of seven-inch baker's spongecake and frosting for outside of cake.

COFFEE-WALNUT SAUCE

1 cup sugar
1½ cups strong coffee
2 tablespoons cornstarch
3 tablespoons cold coffee

2 tablespoons butter
⅓ teaspoon salt
½ cup broken walnut meats

Melt sugar slowly, in heavy skillet, stirring often. Add 1½ cups coffee, slowly and carefully (much steam will rise). Stir constantly. Dissolve cornstarch in cold coffee; stir into warm mixture and continue stirring until sauce boils and thickens. Add butter, salt, and walnuts. Serve warm on ice cream. *Makes about 2 cups.*

STEAK BARBECUE SAUCE

⅔ cup strong coffee
⅓ cup butter or margarine
2 teaspoons Worcestershire sauce
1½ teaspoons dry mustard
1 tablespoon lemon juice
1 teaspoon sugar
Tabasco

Combine all ingredients in saucepan. Heat, stirring until butter melts. Brush over steak as it broils. *Makes about 1 cup.*

Puddings, Parfaits, and Desserts

Come, Nectar divine, inspire thou me,
I wish but Antigone, dessert and thee.

Jacques Delille (1738–1813)
from "Three Reigns of Nature"
(translated from the French)

BAKED INDIAN PUDDING

⅓ cup yellow corn meal
½ teaspoon salt
¼ teaspoon ginger
¼ teaspoon cinnamon
3½ cups milk

½ cup molasses
⅛ teaspoon baking soda
½ cup strong, cold coffee
1 tablespoon butter or
margarine

Combine corn meal, salt, and spices. Scald 2 cups milk and add slowly, stirring constantly. Add molasses and baking soda, mixing thoroughly. Add remaining cold milk and coffee; stir well. Cook over hot water, stirring occasionally, until slightly thickened (about 15 minutes). Pour into greased baking dish. Dot butter or margarine over surface. Set in pan of warm water. Bake in slow oven (300° F), 2 hours and 10 minutes. Serve warm, with coffee ice cream. *Makes 6 servings.*

BRAZILIAN PUDIM MOKA

3 cups milk	½ cup sugar
1 cup light cream	1 teaspoon vanilla
5 tablespoons instant coffee	½ teaspoon salt
2 teaspoons grated orange peel	Nutmeg
	1 cup chopped Brazil nuts
4 eggs plus 1 egg yolk	Royal Chocolate Sauce*

Combine milk and cream; scald. Stir in instant coffee and orange peel. Cool 10 minutes. Beat eggs and egg yolk slightly. Beat in sugar. Add coffee mixture slowly, with vanilla and salt. Strain through fine sieve. Pour into 6 to 8 custard cups, depending on size. Sprinkle with nutmeg. Place cups in baking pan. Fill pan with cold water to within ¾ inch of top of cups. Bake in moderate oven (325° F) for 1 hour or until knife inserted in center comes out clean. Chill. To serve, invert each custard in serving dish. Sprinkle with Brazil nuts. Pour on Royal Chocolate Sauce. *Makes 6 to 8 servings.*

ROYAL CHOCOLATE SAUCE*

2 squares (1 ounce each) unsweetened chocolate	Few grains salt
	3 tablespoons butter or margarine
6 tablespoons water	
½ cup sugar	½ teaspoon vanilla

Combine chocolate and water in saucepan. Stir over low heat until smooth and blended. Add sugar and salt. Stir constantly until sugar is dissolved and mixture slightly thickened. Remove from heat. Stir in butter and vanilla. Stir until blended. *Makes about 1 cup.*

CHRISTMAS PLUM PUDDING

1 cup seedless raisins
1½ cups mixed diced
   candied fruits and peels
½ cup chopped walnuts
1 cup sifted enriched flour,
   divided
2 eggs, beaten
¾ cup molasses
¾ cup buttermilk
½ cup finely chopped suet

¼ cup strong, cold coffee
1 cup fine, dry bread
   crumbs
¾ teaspoon baking soda
¼ teaspoon cloves
¼ teaspoon allspice
¼ teaspoon cinnamon
¼ teaspoon nutmeg
¾ teaspoon salt

Combine raisins, fruits and peels, walnuts and ½ cup of the flour. Combine eggs, molasses, buttermilk, suet, and coffee. Combine remaining flour, crumbs, baking soda, spices, and salt; add to egg mixture. Add floured fruit; mix well. Pour into well-greased 1½-quart mold; set on rack in deep kettle; add boiling water to about one inch below cover of mold. Cover. Steam 1½ to 2 hours. *Makes 10 to 12 servings.*

COFFEE BREAD-AND-BUTTER
PUDDING

1 cup strong coffee
1 cup light cream
2 cups milk
6 thin slices raisin bread
Soft butter or margarine
2 eggs

½ cup sugar
½ teaspoon salt
1 teaspoon vanilla
¼ teaspoon nutmeg

Combine coffee, cream, and milk; bring to scalding point. Spread bread slices lightly with butter or margarine; do not trim off crust. Cut in ½-inch cubes and add to coffee mixture.

Beat eggs slightly; add sugar and salt; mix well. Add bread mixture and vanilla. Pour into 1½-quart casserole. Sprinkle with nutmeg. Set casserole in pan of warm water. Bake in moderate oven (325° F), 1 hour and 15 minutes or until knife inserted near rim of casserole comes out clean. Chill. Serve with plain or whipped cream. *Makes 8 servings.*

COFFEE JELLY WITH VANILLA CUSTARD SAUCE

1 envelope unflavored   ⅛ teaspoon salt
   gelatin   1 teaspoon pure vanilla
¼ cup cold water   extract
2 teaspoons instant coffee   Vanilla Custard Sauce*
1¾ cups hot water   Whipped cream
¼ cup sugar

Soften gelatin in cold water. Dissolve instant coffee in hot water and add to softened gelatin. Stir in sugar, salt, and pure vanilla extract. Chill until firm and ready to serve in an 8-inch-square pan or in an ice-cube tray. To serve: cut into cubes and spoon into sherbet glasses with alternate layers of Vanilla Custard Sauce. Top with whipped cream. *Makes 4 to 5 servings.*

VANILLA CUSTARD SAUCE*

3 tablespoons sugar   1 cup milk
⅛ teaspoon salt   ¾ teaspoon pure vanilla
1 egg   extract

Combine sugar and salt in a small saucepan. Beat in egg. Stir in milk. Cook over low heat, stirring constantly, until custard coats a metal spoon. Chill. Stir in pure vanilla extract. *Makes 1 cup.*

COTTAGE PUDDING WITH COFFEE-TOFFEE SAUCE

1 *package spice-cake mix*
1 *cup firmly packed brown sugar*
1½ *cups strong, hot coffee*

2 *tablespoons cornstarch*
3 *tablespoons cold coffee*
2 *tablespoons butter*
2 *teaspoons vanilla*

Prepare cake mix as directed on package. Bake in 13×9×2-inch oblong pan as directed. Meanwhile, combine brown sugar and hot coffee. Stir over low heat until sugar melts. Blend cornstarch and add cold coffee; stir in. Cook and stir until sauce boils and thickens. Remove from heat. Add butter and vanilla. Stir until butter dissolves. Serve warm, over squares of warm cake. *Makes 12 servings.*

JELLIED COFFEE SOUFFLE

1½ *cups strong coffee*
½ *cup milk*
1 *envelope unflavored gelatin*
¼ *cup cold water*
3 *eggs, separated*

⅔ *cup sugar*
¼ *teaspoon salt*
½ *teaspoon vanilla*
½ *cup heavy cream, whipped*

Scald coffee and milk in top of double boiler. Sprinkle gelatin on cold water; let stand five minutes and dissolve in hot-coffee mixture. Beat egg yolks in a mixing bowl, adding 1 tablespoon sugar and salt while beating. Add hot-coffee mixture slowly to egg yolks. Return to double boiler; stir over hot (not boiling) water, until mixture coats spoon. Cool. Chill until consistency of unbeaten egg white. Beat egg whites stiff; beat in remaining sugar and vanilla. Fold into gelatin mixture; beat until smooth. Fold in whipped cream. Turn into mold and chill until set. Unmold, garnish with whipped cream and cubes of plain coffee jelly. *Makes 6 servings.*

A characteristic group of Britishers taking coffee in the time of Charles II.

MOCHA COTTAGE PUDDING

¼ cup shortening
½ cup sugar
1 egg, well beaten
1½ squares (1 ounce each) unsweetened chocolate, melted
1¾ cups sifted enriched flour

2 teaspoons baking powder
½ teaspoon salt
¼ cup evaporated milk
½ cup strong, cold coffee
⅛ teaspoon baking soda
Fluffy Vanilla Sauce*

Cream shortening and sugar, add egg and beat well. Add melted chocolate. Mix and sift flour, baking powder, and salt. Combine evaporated milk, coffee, and baking soda. Add flour mixture and coffee mixture alternately to chocolate mixture. Bake in greased 9-inch-square cake pan in moderate oven (350° F) for 40 minutes or until done. Serve warm with Fluffy Vanilla Sauce. *Makes 9 squares.*

FLUFFY VANILLA SAUCE*

Combine 1 cup sugar and ⅓ cup water in saucepan. Stir over low heat until sugar dissolves. Cook to 238° F or soft-ball stage. Beat 2 egg yolks until thick and lemon-colored. Pour syrup slowly on yolks while beating. Continue to beat until creamy. Chill. Add 1 tablespoon vanilla. Whip 1 cup heavy cream and fold in.

MOCHA-WALNUT STEAMED PUDDING

3 tablespoons shortening
⅔ cup sugar
1 egg, well beaten
2¼ cups sifted cake flour
3 teaspoons baking powder
¼ teaspoon salt
½ cup evaporated milk

½ cup strong coffee
⅛ teaspoon baking soda
3 squares (1 ounce each) unsweetened chocolate, melted
½ cup chopped walnuts
1 teaspoon vanilla

Cream shortening and sugar; add egg. Mix and sift flour, baking powder, and salt; combine evaporated milk, coffee, and baking soda. Add flour mixture and coffee mixture alternately to egg mixture. Add melted chocolate and vanilla. Stir in walnuts. Fill greased mold two thirds full. Cover; steam one hour. *Makes 8 servings.*

PUDDING PARFAIT

1 *package vanilla pudding*
mix
½ *cup heavy cream*
¼ *cup sugar*

½ *teaspoon pure vanilla*
extract
1 *teaspoon instant coffee*

Prepare pudding according to direction on package. Cool. Combine heavy cream, sugar, pure vanilla extract, and instant coffee. Beat until stiff. Spoon pudding alternately with cream mixture into 6 parfait glasses. Chill. *Makes 6 servings.*

BIMINI PARFAIT

Fill dessert glasses about one third with vanilla ice cream. Add a layer of Coffee-Caramel Sauce, then a layer of Fudge Sauce. Fill with ice cream. Add more Fudge Sauce. Top with whipped cream and instant coffee.

COFFEE-CARAMEL SAUCE*

¾ *cup brown sugar, firmly*
packed
1 *cup sugar*
⅔ *cup light corn syrup*
¼ *cup butter or margarine*

Few grains salt
⅓ *cup cream*
½ *teaspoon vanilla*
½ *cup strong coffee*

Combine first 5 ingredients in saucepan. Cook, stirring, until sugar dissolves. Cook without stirring to 236° F or softball stage. Cool slightly. Stir in cream, vanilla, and coffee; mix well. *Makes about 2 cups.*

FUDGE SAUCE*

4 squares (1 ounce each)
unsweetened chocolate
1 cup sugar
2 tablespoons butter or
margarine

2 small cans evaporated
milk
2 teaspoons vanilla

Melt chocolate over hot water. Stir in sugar gradually. Add butter, stir until melted. Stir in evaporated milk slowly. Cook over hot water, stirring often, until thickened. Add vanilla and cool. *Makes 2 cups.*

COFFEE-ALMOND PARFAIT

1 pint coffee ice cream
½ cup chopped, toasted
almonds

Butterscotch Sauce*
½ cup heavy cream,
whipped

Fill 4 parfait glasses with alternating layers of ice cream, almonds, Butterscotch Sauce, and whipped cream. *Makes 4 servings.*

BUTTERSCOTCH SAUCE*

1 cup brown sugar, firmly
packed
¼ cup light cream
2 tablespoons light corn
syrup

3 tablespoons butter
½ teaspoon vanilla

Combine brown sugar, cream, corn syrup, and butter in deep saucepan. Bring to a boil, stirring constantly. Boil without stirring 3 minutes. Remove from heat; add vanilla; cool. *Makes 4 to 6 servings.*

COFFEE-TAPIOCA PARFAIT

1 *egg, separated*
5 *tablespoons sugar,*
   divided
2 *cups warm coffee*
3 *tablespoons quick-cooking*
   tapioca

⅛ *teaspoon salt*
½ *teaspoon vanilla*
1 *cup heavy cream, whipped*
Chocolate syrup
Chopped walnuts

Beat egg white until foamy. Add 2 tablespoons sugar, singly, beating until mixture forms soft peaks. Set aside. Combine egg yolk with ¼ cup coffee in saucepan. Add tapioca, salt, remaining coffee and sugar. Stir over medium heat until mixture comes to full boil (5 to 8 minutes). Remove from heat; pour small amount on egg-white mixture and blend well. Quickly stir in remaining tapioca mixture; add vanilla. Cool; stir once after 15 minutes. Chill. Spoon alternate layers of tapioca mixture, whipped cream, and chocolate syrup into parfait glasses. Top with whipped cream and chopped walnuts. *Makes 6 to 8 servings.*

VANILLA-COFFEE-JELLY PARFAIT

1 *envelope unflavored*
   gelatin
¼ *cup strong, cold coffee*
2 *cups strong, hot coffee*

½ *cup sugar*
1 *tablespoon vanilla*
1 *package dessert topping,*
   whipped

Soften gelatin in cold coffee; dissolve in hot coffee. Add sugar; stir until dissolved. Cool and add vanilla. Chill until slightly thickened. Reserve enough whipped topping for garnish; fold remainder into thickened coffee jelly until a marbled effect is obtained. Spoon into parfait glasses. Garnish with reserve topping. *Makes 4 to 6 servings, depending on size of glasses.*

COFFEE-BANANA SHERBET

1 junket (rennet) tablet
1 tablespoon cold water
2 cups skim milk
½ cup sugar
1/16 teaspoon salt

½ teaspoon instant coffee
1 large banana
1½ teaspoons pure vanilla
extract

Crush junket (rennet) tablet and dissolve in cold water. Combine next 4 ingredients and heat to lukewarm, stirring constantly. Test a drop on the inside of the wrist frequently. When comfortably warm (110° F) remove from heat at once. Add dissolved junket tablet. Stir a few seconds only. Pour at once, while still liquid, into an ice-cube tray. DO NOT DISTURB FOR 10 MINUTES WHILE MILK SETS. Place in a freezer and freeze until almost firm. Turn mixture into a bowl, break up with a fork and beat with an electric or rotary beater until fluffy and free from lumps. Add mashed banana and pure vanilla extract. Beat until well blended. Return to freezing tray and freeze until firm. *Makes 8 servings.*

BANANA FRITTERS
WITH COFFEE-RUM SAUCE

1 cup sifted enriched flour
2 teaspoons baking powder
1¼ teaspoons salt
¼ cup sugar
1 egg, well beaten

⅓ cup milk
2 teaspoons melted
shortening
2 to 3 firm bananas
Coffee-Rum Sauce*

Mix and sift flour, baking powder, salt, and sugar. Combine egg, milk, and melted shortening; add to dry ingredients and mix smooth. (This is a very stiff batter; DO NOT THIN IT DOWN. It will stay crisp after frying for 15 to 20 minutes.) Cut each banana crosswise into 3 or 4 even pieces; roll in flour; coat with fritter batter. Fry in shallow fat, two inches deep (375° F) about 5 minutes, or until well browned. Turn often to brown evenly. Drain on a rack. Serve hot with Coffee-Rum Sauce. *Makes 8 to 12 fritters.*

COFFEE-RUM SAUCE*

1 cup sugar
1½ cups strong coffee
2 tablespoons cornstarch
3 tablespoons cold coffee

2 tablespoons butter or margarine
½ to 1 teaspoon rum flavoring (to taste)

Melt sugar slowly in heavy skillet, stirring often. Add coffee slowly, stirring constantly. Blend cornstarch and cold coffee; stir in. Continue to cook and stir until sauce boils and thickens. Remove from heat; add butter and flavoring; stir until butter dissolves. *Makes 2 cups.*

BRAZILIAN COFFEE SUNDAE

¼ cup butter, at room temperature
¾ cup sugar
2 eggs, at room temperature
½ cup ice water
½ cup instant nonfat dry milk crystals
1½ teaspoons vanilla

1 tablespoon instant coffee powder
2 tablespoons lemon juice
1 cup guava or apricot jam, melted
2½ cups coffee whipped instant nonfat dry milk crystals
Fresh peach slices

Make coffee ice cream as follows: with electric mixer cream butter and sugar until light and fluffy. Add eggs, one at a time, beating well after each addition. Beat at high speed for about 5 minutes. Mix water, instant crystals, vanilla, coffee powder, in bowl. Whip until soft peaks form, about 3 to 4 minutes. Add lemon juice and continue whipping until stiff peaks form, 3 to 4 minutes longer. Fold into ice cream. Turn into refrigerator trays. Freeze until firm. At serving time scoop out 8 portions of coffee ice cream. Top with melted guava jelly and coffee whipped instant crystals. Garnish with peach slices. *Makes 8 servings.*

To whip coffee instant nonfat dry milk crystals: mix ½ cup instant nonfat dry milk crystals, ½ cup ice water, and 1 tablespoon instant coffee powder in bowl. Whip until soft peaks form (about 3 to 4 minutes). Add 2 tablespoons lemon juice. Continue whipping until stiff peaks form (3 to 4 minutes longer). Gradually add ¼ cup sugar. *Makes about 2½ cups.*

CAFE GLACEE

4 egg yolks
4 tablespoons sugar

1 cup double-strength, cold coffee
2 cups heavy cream

Place small mixing bowl in large bowl filled with hot water. Larger bowl should act as water jacket. Put egg yolks, sugar, and coffee in smaller bowl. Beat ingredients until mixture is light and creamy. Whip cream until stiff. Add to coffee mixture and mix well. Pour into mold. Place in refrigerator until well chilled. *Makes 4 to 6 servings.*

COFFEE-BANANA ICE CREAM

1 package instant vanilla
  pudding mix
½ cup strong coffee
½ cup mashed ripe
  banana

1 cup heavy cream
Chopped pistachio nuts
  (optional)

Follow recipe for ice cream as given on package of pudding mix, substituting coffee, banana, and heavy cream for liquid called for in recipe. Freeze as directed. Garnish with chopped pistachio nuts, if desired. *Makes 4 to 6 servings.*

COFFEE BOATS

2 fresh pineapples
1 cantaloupe
¼ cup maraschino cordial
¼ cup Cointreau cordial

1 quart coffee ice cream
¼ cup shredded coconut
½ pint whipping cream,
whipped

Cut pineapples in half, lengthwise; scoop out, leaving border about ½ inch thick. Cut pineapple scoopings into small pieces. Cut cantaloupe in half; remove rind, seeds. Cut cantaloupe into small pieces. Combine maraschino and Cointreau cordials; add pineapple, cantaloupe pieces; let stand 3 hours. Spoon fruit into pineapple shells; top each shell with two scoops of coffee ice cream. Sprinkle with shredded coconut; garnish with whipped cream. *Makes 4 servings.*

COFFEE-BRANDY ICE CREAM

1 cup cold double-strength
coffee
½ cup brandy

2 cups heavy cream
2 cups light cream

Pour all ingredients into mixing bowl. Mix well. Pour into freezer tray. Freeze until firm. *Makes 6 servings.*

COFFEE CHARLOTTE

2 envelopes unflavored
gelatin
1 cup milk
1 cup strong coffee
1 cup sugar, divided
2 egg whites

⅛ teaspoon salt
2 cups whipping cream,
divided
4 to 5 dozen ladyfingers
Candy coffee beans
(optional)

Soften gelatin in cold milk. Heat coffee to boiling point and add to milk mixture. Stir until gelatin dissolves. Stir in ¾ cup sugar and stir until sugar dissolves. Chill until slightly thickened. Whip egg whites until soft peaks form. Add remaining ¼ cup sugar and salt gradually, beating until stiff and glossy. Fold into gelatin mixture. Whip 1½ cups cream; fold in. Line 8 dessert glasses with ladyfingers. Spoon gelatin mixture into glasses. Chill until set. Whip remaining cream. Use as garnish with candy coffee beans. *Makes 8 servings.*

The Café Foy in the Palais Royal, 1789 (from an engraving by Bos Redon).

CAFE-CREME FROMAGE

1 envelope unflavored gelatin	1 package (8-ounce) cream cheese
½ cup strong, cold coffee, divided	2 egg whites
½ cup boiling water	¼ cup sugar
	Spiced, fresh peaches

Soften gelatin in ¼ cup of the cold coffee and add boiling water. Stir until dissolved. Stir in remaining coffee. Beat cream cheese until soft and beat into gelatin mixture. Chill until slightly thickened. Beat egg whites stiff and add sugar gradually while beating. Fold into gelatin mixture. Spoon into 4 to 6 individual molds and chill until set. Serve with spiced, fresh peaches. *Makes 4 to 6 servings.*

COFFEE-DOUGHNUT CUSTARD

3 tablespoons butter or margarine	½ teaspoon salt
4 eggs, slightly beaten	½ teaspoon nutmeg
2½ cups milk, scalded	2 teaspoons vanilla
2½ cups strong coffee	8 packaged cinnamon doughnuts
⅔ cup sugar	

Melt butter. Combine with eggs, milk, coffee, sugar, salt, nutmeg, and vanilla. Stir until sugar dissolves. Pour into buttered 2-quart casserole. Float doughnuts on top. Set casserole in pan of hot water. Bake at 350° F for 1 hour, or until knife inserted near edge comes out clean. Chill. *Makes 8 servings.*

COFFEE-GLAZED BAKED APPLES

6 large baking apples
1½ cups brown sugar
½ cup chopped walnuts

1 cup strong coffee
Whipped cream

Select 6 large baking apples. Core. Peel about ⅓ of the way down from stem end. Combine ½ cup brown sugar and chopped walnuts. Fill apples with this mixture. Set in baking pan. Combine remaining 1 cup brown sugar, and coffee. Stir over low heat until sugar melts, then simmer 10 minutes. Pour over apples. Bake in moderate oven (375° F), 30 minutes, or until almost tender, basting frequently with syrup in pan. Remove from oven. Sprinkle peeled surface with a little sugar. Place under broiler about 4 inches below source of heat. Sprinkle frequently with sugar and baste with syrup until apples are glazed, about 15 minutes. Serve warm or cold with whipped cream.

COFFEE JELLY WITH BANANAS

2 envelopes unflavored
   gelatin
3 cups strong, hot coffee
3 tablespoons sherry

⅓ cup strong, cold coffee
½ cup sugar
2 bananas, cut in ½-inch
   slices

Soften gelatin in cold coffee; dissolve in hot coffee. Add sugar, stirring until dissolved; add sherry. Chill until set. Place sliced bananas in serving dishes, cover with coffee jelly. Serve with light cream. *Makes 6 servings.*

COFFEE-MACAROON DESSERT

2 envelopes unflavored
    gelatin
½ cup cold water
2 cups double-strength, hot
    coffee

½ cup sugar
1½ cups heavy cream
1 cup macaroon crumbs

Sprinkle gelatin on cold water to soften. Pour into hot coffee. Add sugar when gelatin is dissolved. Allow to cool. Whip cream until stiff. Mix in macaroon crumbs. Add coffee mixture and mix well. Place in refrigerator to chill thoroughly. *Makes 6 servings.*

COFFEE
AND MARSHMALLOW DESSERT

1 cup double-strength, hot coffee
24 large marshmallows, cut up
1 cup heavy cream

Pour coffee in saucepan. Add marshmallows. Cook slowly over low flame, stirring until marshmallows are dissolved. Remove and chill. Whip cream stiff. Fold whipped cream into chilled marshmallows. Place in refrigerator for several hours before serving. *Makes 4 servings.*

COFFEE MOUSSE

2 cups heavy cream
⅓ cup ground coffee
1 teaspoon vanilla

½ cup extra-fine
    granulated sugar
Few grains salt

Combine ½ cup cream and coffee in top of double boiler. Heat over boiling water 10 minutes. Strain through cheesecloth or fine sieve. Whip remaining cream until it forms soft mound. Add sugar, salt, vanilla, and coffee mixture. Freeze in trays of automatic refrigerator. Freeze firm, without stirring. *Makes 8 servings.*

COFFEE PARADISE

1 envelope unflavored
  gelatin
2 tablespoons cold water
6 tablespoons sugar
1 cup strong, hot coffee

½ cup pear syrup
5 to 6 canned pear halves
1 cup heavy cream,
  whipped
¼ teaspoon vanilla

Soften gelatin in cold water. Add sugar; pour hot coffee over all and stir until dissolved. Add pear syrup. Arrange pear halves in bottom of 10-inch ring mold. Add part of gelatin mixture to a depth of about half an inch and chill. Chill remaining gelatin mixture until slightly thickened. Whip cream and vanilla together and fold into gelatin mixture. Spoon into ring mold and chill until firm. Unmold on serving platter. Serve with additional whipped cream, if desired, and chocolate sauce. *Makes 6 to 8 servings.*

COFFEE TORTONI

1 egg white
1 tablespoon instant coffee
⅛ teaspoon salt
2 tablespoons sugar
1 cup heavy cream
¼ cup sugar

1 teaspoon vanilla
⅛ teaspoon almond
  extract
¼ cup toasted almonds,
  finely chopped

Set control of refrigerator at coldest point. Combine egg white, coffee, and salt. Beat until stiff but not dry. Add 2 tablespoons sugar gradually. Beat until stiff and satiny. Combine cream, ¼ cup sugar, vanilla, and almond extract. Beat until stiff. Fold in egg-white mixture and almonds. Pour into eight 2-ounce paper cups. Freeze until firm. *Makes 8 servings.*

COFFEE-VANILLA MILK SHERBET

1 junket (rennet) tablet
1 tablespoon cold water
2 cups skim milk
½ cup sugar
1/16 teaspoon salt
1½ teaspoons pure vanilla
  extract

2½ teaspoons instant
  coffee
2 tablespoons light corn
  syrup

Crush rennet tablet and dissolve in the cold water. Combine the remaining ingredients, mix well and heat to lukewarm, stirring constantly. Test a drop of the mixture on the inside of the wrist frequently. When comfortably warm (110° F) remove from heat at once. Add dissolved rennet tablet. Stir a few seconds *only.* Pour at once, while still liquid, into an ice-cube tray. DO NOT DISTURB FOR 10 MINUTES WHILE MILK SETS. Place in freezing compartment of the refrigerator and freeze until almost firm. Remove from tray; break up with a fork and beat with an electric or rotary beater until fluffy and free from lumps but still a thick mush. Return to ice-cube tray and freeze until firm. *Makes 8 servings.*

COUPE CURACAO

COUPE CRUSTS:

3 egg whites
½ cup milk

¾ cup sugar
¾ cup all-purpose flour

FILLING:

Tropical fruit, diced, such
  as pineapple or banana
1 quart vanilla ice cream
1 quart coffee ice cream
6 ounces Curaçao liqueur
1 cup butterscotch sauce

½ cup whipping cream,
  whipped
6 maraschino cherries
¼ square unsweetened
  chocolate, shaved

Combine egg whites, milk, sugar, flour; mix well. Pour enough batter (approximately ¼ cup) to form a 5-inch "pancake" on a well-greased cookie sheet. Bake two coupe crusts at a time on a cookie sheet for 4 to 5 minutes at 500° F, until edges of crust become golden brown. Remove coupe crusts immediately from cookie sheet. Place each crust over 4-ounce custard cup; press another custard cup on top to make a coupe. Remove custard cups immediately from coupe. Cool. Fill each coupe with diced tropical fruit. Pour one ounce of Curaçao liqueur over fruit in each coupe. Top with one scoop each of vanilla and coffee ice cream. Pour butterscotch sauce over all. Decorate with whipped cream, maraschino cherry, shaved chocolate. *Makes 6 servings.*

FRENCH-CHOCOLATE
AND COFFEE-CHIFFON CREAM

1½ cups milk
3 eggs, separated
½ cup sugar, divided
2 teaspoons flour
⅛ teaspoon salt
½ teaspoon ground
  allspice

2 squares (1 ounce each)
  semisweet chocolate
1 tablespoon strong, cold
  coffee
½ teaspoon pure vanilla
  extract
Ladyfingers

Scald milk. Combine 2 to 3 tablespoons scalded milk with egg yolks, ¼ cup sugar, flour, salt, and allspice. Mix well.

Add to remaining milk; cook over low heat or hot water until custard coats a metal spoon, stirring constantly. Remove from heat. Melt chocolate and add to custard along with coffee and vanilla extract. Cool. Beat egg whites until they form soft peaks. Add remaining ¼ cup sugar gradually, beating until stiff. Fold into chocolate custard. Chill. Serve in sherbet glasses, lined with ladyfingers. Garnish with whipped cream, if desired. *Makes 4 servings.*

GINGER-COFFEE REFRIGERATOR DESSERT

½ cup butter or margarine　Gingersnaps
1¼ cups sifted　　　　　　1 tablespoon strong, cold
　confectioners' sugar　　　coffee
4 egg yolks　　　　　　　　1 teaspoon rum flavoring
¼ cup strong, cold coffee

Cream butter or margarine until light and fluffy. Beat in sugar gradually. Add egg yolks, one at a time, beating well. Blend in ¼ cup coffee. Line a loaf pan with waxed paper. Arrange layer of gingersnaps on bottom. Combine 1 tablespoon coffee with rum flavoring; sprinkle a little on gingersnaps. Add a layer of filling, then one of gingersnaps, sprinkled with coffee-rum-flavoring mixture. Continue until filling is used, ending with gingersnaps. Chill overnight. *Makes 6 servings.*

GLACE A LA MERE

2 quarts coffee ice cream　Chocolate Whipped
1 quart chocolate ice　　　Cream*
　cream
½ cup heavy cream,
　whipped

Line bottom and sides of 9-cup mold with coffee ice cream. Fill center with chocolate ice cream. Freeze firm. Run spatula around rim and invert on serving plate. Place hot, damp cloth on top and shake gently until mold slips out. Garnish base with plain whipped cream and Chocolate Whipped Cream.

CHOCOLATE WHIPPED CREAM *

½ cup whipping cream
¼ teaspoon vanilla
Few grains salt

2 tablespoons sugar
2 tablespoons cocoa

Combine all ingredients in small bowl. Chill for half an hour. Whip with rotary egg beater until stiff enough to hold its shape.

MOCHA BRAZIL-NUT ICE CREAM

1 envelope unflavored
   gelatin
¼ cup cold water
1 cup strong, hot coffee
1 square (1 ounce)
   unsweetened chocolate,
   melted
¾ cup light-brown sugar

¼ teaspoon salt
1 teaspoon vanilla
1 tall (14½ ounce) can
   evaporated milk
1½ cups heavy cream
¾ cup chopped, roasted
   Brazil nuts (unsalted)

Soften gelatin in cold water; dissolve in hot coffee; add slowly to melted chocolate, blending well. Add brown sugar and salt; stir until sugar dissolves. Cool. Add vanilla, evaporated milk, and cream (not whipped). Pour into refrigerator freezing trays. Freeze to a stiff mush. Stir in Brazil nuts. Freeze firm. Garnish with Brazil nut chips if desired. *Makes 8 servings.*

MOCHA-DATE DESSERT

1 envelope unflavored
  gelatin
¼ cup cold water
1 cup strong, hot coffee
⅓ cup sugar
2 tablespoons instant
  cocoa

¼ teaspoon salt
1 cup pitted dates, sliced
¼ cup chopped walnuts
½ cup heavy cream,
  whipped
½ teaspoon vanilla

Sprinkle gelatin on cold water. Add coffee; stir until gelatin dissolves. Mix sugar, cocoa, and salt; add; stir until dissolved. Chill until consistency of unbeaten egg white; fold in dates, nuts, whipped cream, and vanilla. Turn into mold; chill until firm. Unmold; garnish with whipped cream.

MOCHA ICE CREAM

¼ cup butter, at room
  temperature
¾ cup sugar
2 eggs, at room
  temperature
2 squares (1 ounce each)
  unsweetened chocolate,
  melted and cooled

½ cup ice water
½ cup instant nonfat dry
  milk crystals
1½ teaspoons vanilla
1 tablespoon instant coffee
2 tablespoons lemon juice

Using electric mixer, cream butter and sugar until light and fluffy. Add eggs, one at a time, beating well after each addition. Beat at high speed 5 minutes. Beat in chocolate. Mix ice water, instant crystals, vanilla, and instant coffee in bowl; whip until soft peaks form (3 to 4 minutes). Add lemon juice and continue whipping until stiff peaks form (3 to 4 minutes longer). Fold whipped crystals into chocolate mixture. Freeze. *Makes about 1 quart.*

MOCHA MOUSSE

1 *cup double-strength, hot*
coffee
6 *tablespoons grated bitter*
chocolate

2 *cups heavy cream*
½ *cup sugar*

Pour coffee in saucepan. Place over low heat. Add chocolate and stir until chocolate is dissolved. Remove from heat and

The caffè Biffi-Scala. For almost two centuries this elegant spot has flourished under the patronage of Milanese high society.

cool. Combine cream and sugar in mixing bowl. Beat until stiff. Mix in cool mocha. Turn into mold. Place in refrigerator. *Makes 4 to 6 servings.*

MOCHA-SNOW DESSERT

1 cup sifted flour
1 cup sugar
½ teaspoon salt
⅔ cup soft butter or
  margarine
1 tablespoon instant coffee
2 eggs
2 squares (1 ounce each)
  unsweetened chocolate,
  melted

½ cup chopped walnuts
1 7-ounce package (2
  cups) miniature
  marshmallows
1 6-ounce package (1 cup)
  semisweet chocolate
  pieces

Combine and sift flour, sugar, and salt. Add butter or margarine, coffee and eggs; beat thoroughly. Add chocolate and walnuts. Blend well. Pour into greased 9-inch-square pan. Bake at 350° F for 30 minutes. Cover with marshmallows; bake 2 minutes longer. Melt chocolate pieces over hot (not boiling) water. Spread over marshmallow. Serve warm or cold. *Makes 10 to 12 servings.*

PECAN-COFFEE DELIGHT

1 quart coffee ice cream
1 cup chopped pecans
½ cup moist flaked
  coconut

2 tablespoons Kahlúa or
  Cointreau liqueur

Soften ice cream slightly. Working quickly, blend pecans, coconut, and liqueur into softened ice cream; pack mixture into cold ice-cube trays or chilled container. Place in ice-cube compartment or freezer to harden. Slice and serve with a splash of the same liqueur used in mixture. *Makes 6 servings.*

VANILLA-BANANA COFFEE CREAM

1 egg
1 egg yolk
4 tablespoons sugar
¼ teaspoon salt
4 teaspoons instant coffee
2 cups skim milk
1 envelope unflavored
  gelatin

¼ cup cold water
1 medium banana, mashed
  (½ cup)
1½ teaspoons pure vanilla
  extract
1 egg white

Beat egg and yolk lightly in top of double boiler. Combine 3 tablespoons of the sugar, salt, and coffee; mix with the egg. Stir in milk and cook over low heat or hot water until the mixture begins to thicken (15 to 20 minutes), stirring constantly. Soften gelatin in cold water and stir into the hot custard. Chill until the mixture begins to thicken. Beat in banana and pure vanilla extract. Beat egg white until it stands in soft peaks into which gradually beat remaining 1 tablespoon sugar. Fold into the mixture. Pour into 6 individual molds and chill until firm. *Makes 6 servings.*

"Coffee and . . ." Favorites Around the World

"Coffee and . . ." is the introduction to a phrase commonly used whether the "and" is followed by apple pie in America, Linzertorte in Austria, brioche in France, or Vetebröd in Sweden. From Johann Sebastian Bach's secular cantata No. 211, called the "Coffee Cantata," to the popular American Song, "Let's Have Another Cup of Coffee," the praises of this brew have been acclaimed in song and poetry through the centuries.

> For lo! the board with cups and spoons is crowned,
> The berries crackle, and the mill turns round;
> On shining Altars of Japan they raise
> The silver lamp; the fiery spirits blaze:
> From silver spouts the grateful liquors glide,
> While China's earth receives the smoking tide:
> At once they gratify their scent and taste,
> And frequent cups prolong the rich repast.
> Straight hover round the Fair her airy band;
> Some, as she sipped, the fuming liquor fanned,
> Some o'er her lap their careful plumes displayed,
> Trembling, and conscious of the rich brocade.
> Coffee (which makes the politician wise,
> And see through all things with his half-shut eyes),
> Sent up in vapors to the Baron's brain
> New Stratagems, the radiant Lock to gain.

Alexander Pope (1688–1744)
from Canto III "The Rape of the Lock"

APPLE PIE
(America)

6 to 8 large tart apples
2 (9-inch) unbaked pie
    crusts
½ cup granulated sugar
½ cup dark-brown sugar
1 tablespoon flour
½ teaspoon nutmeg,
    grated

Grated peel of one orange
Grated peel of one lemon
2 tablespoons orange juice
3 tablespoons butter or
    margarine

Pare and core apples. Cut each in 8 or 10 slices, depending on size. Line a deep nine-inch pan with one pie crust. Combine sugars, flour, and nutmeg. Rub a little of this mixture into pastry lining. Add grated peels to remaining sugar mixture. Arrange sliced apples in pan, sprinkling each layer with some of the sugar mixture. Sprinkle the whole with orange juice. Dot apples with butter. Fit top crust over apple layers, pressing the edges together or fluting them. Cut slit in top crust to release steam, and bake in hot oven (425° F), 40 to 45 minutes or until tender. Serve warm, topped with vanilla ice cream. *Makes one 9-inch pie.*

CAMPAIGN MOLASSES CAKE
(A Civil War Favorite)
(America)

5½ cups all-purpose flour,
    sifted
2 teaspoons salt
4 teaspoons baking powder
1 teaspoon baking soda
2 teaspoons ginger
4 teaspoons cinnamon

1 teaspoon cloves
1 cup shortening
1 cup sugar
2 cups molasses
4 eggs
2 cups hot water

Mix and sift flour, salt, baking powder, baking soda, ginger, cinnamon, and cloves. Cream shortening and sugar. Blend in molasses. Stir in ½ cup flour mixture; beat in eggs. Add hot water alternately with remaining flour mixture. Turn into greased and waxed-paper-lined 8×12×2-inch pan. Bake in moderate oven (350° F), 50 to 60 minutes. Cool. Cut into squares.

CHEESE BREAD
(America)

¾ cup boiling water
½ cup seedless raisins
1¾ cups enriched flour, sifted
½ teaspoon salt

1 teaspoon baking soda
⅓ cup sugar
1 egg, beaten
1 cup grated sharp Cheddar cheese

Pour boiling water over raisins; let stand 5 minutes. Meanwhile, mix and sift flour, salt, baking soda, and sugar. Add raisins and water; mix well. Add egg and cheese; beat well. Bake in a greased 8-inch tube pan (plain or Turk's Head) in moderate oven (350° F), 50 minutes.

DOUGHNUTS

1 pound vegetable shortening
2⅔ cups sifted flour
4 teaspoons double-acting baking powder
1 teaspoon salt
½ cup sugar

¼ teaspoon nutmeg
½ teaspoon cinnamon
2 eggs, well beaten
½ cup milk
1 teaspoon vanilla
3 tablespoons melted shortening

Heat 1 pound vegetable shortening to 365° F (cube of bread browns in 60 seconds). Sift dry ingredients together. Combine eggs, milk, and vanilla. Add liquid to dry ingredients. Add melted shortening. Mix just to moisten dry ingredients thoroughly. Roll out ¼ inch thick on a floured board. Cut with a doughnut cutter, and fry in hot shortening. Do not fry more than 3 or 4 at a time or fat will cool too rapidly. Fry 3 to 5 minutes or until delicately brown. Turn once. Drain well. Place on absorbent paper. *Makes 20 doughnuts (using 2½-inch cutter).*

INDIVIDUAL COFFEECAKES
(America)

¼ cup shortening	½ teaspoon salt
1⅓ cups sugar, divided	½ cup milk
2 egg yolks	2 egg whites
1¼ cups flour, sifted	½ teaspoon cinnamon
2 teaspoons baking powder	½ cup chopped walnuts

Cream shortening. Add 1 cup of the sugar gradually and cream thoroughly. Beat egg yolks. Add to first mixture. Mix and sift flour, baking powder, and salt; add alternately with milk. Beat egg whites stiff but not dry. Fold in. Pour into well-greased, individual piepans. Mix ⅓ cup sugar with cinnamon and chopped walnuts. Sprinkle over batter. Bake in moderate oven (375° F), 20 to 25 minutes. Serve hot. *Makes 8 servings.*

NEW ORLEANS BIEGNETS
(America)

¼ cup milk	1 egg, beaten
¼ cup sugar	3 cups flour, sifted
1 teaspoon salt	(about)
¼ cup shortening	Confectioners' sugar
1 package dry active yeast	
¼ cup very warm water	
(110°–115° F)	

Scald milk; stir in sugar, salt, and shortening; cool to lukewarm. Sprinkle yeast into very warm water; stir until dissolved. Add lukewarm-milk mixture, egg, and half the flour. Beat well with mixer or spoon for one minute. Add remaining flour and more if needed to make soft dough. Turn out onto lightly floured surface; knead until smooth and elastic. Place in greased bowl; cover and let rise in warm place, free from draft, until doubled, about 1 hour. Punch down and let rise again about ½ hour. Roll out into square a scant ½ inch thick. Cut into 2½- to 3-inch squares. Place on greased baking sheet; let rise until light, about 1 hour. Do not handle while rising or squares will fall. Fry in deep fat, heated to 375° F, for 2 minutes or until brown on each side; drain on absorbent paper. Serve piping hot, sprinkled generously with confectioners' sugar. *Makes about 2 dozen.*

SAVANNAH BREAD
(America)

1¾ cups enriched flour,
  sifted
2 teaspoons baking powder
½ teaspoon salt
¼ teaspoon baking soda
⅓ cup shortening
¾ cup crunchy peanut
  butter

⅔ cup sugar
2 eggs, slightly beaten
1 cup mashed ripe
  bananas (2 to 3
  medium bananas)

Mix and sift first 4 ingredients. Cream shortening and peanut butter. Add sugar gradually while creaming. Continue to cream until light and fluffy. Add eggs and beat well. Stir in dry ingredients alternately with mashed bananas. Mix well, but do not beat. Spoon batter into well-greased, 9×5×3-inch loaf pan. Bake in moderate oven (350°F), 1 hour or until center tests done and loaf pulls away slightly from sides of pan. Cool on cake rack. This bread will stay fresh for almost a week.

LINZERTORTE
(Austria)

1 cup butter or margarine	½ teaspoon cloves
1 cup sugar	¼ teaspoon salt
1 tablespoon grated	1 cup ground nuts
orange or lemon peel	(filberts, almonds, or
2 egg yolks	walnuts)
1½ cups flour, sifted	1 cup plum preserves
1 teaspoon baking powder	Whipped cream
2 teaspoons cinnamon	

Cream butter; add sugar slowly while continuing to cream. Add orange or lemon peel. Add egg yolks one at a time, beating well after each addition. Mix and sift flour, baking powder, spices, and salt. Add slowly, stirring in. Stir in nuts. After all is added, mix with hands until all ingredients are thoroughly combined. Chill. Pat ⅔ of dough into bottom of 9-inch layer-cake pan (preferably one with removable bottom). Spread preserves over this layer. Roll out remaining dough; cut into 8 strips ¾ inch wide and place lattice fashion on top of preserves. Bake in moderate oven (350° F) for 50 to 60 minutes or until edges of strips recede from sides of pan. Remove from pan. Cool. Garnish with a frill of whipped cream. Cut into small wedges to serve. *Makes 10 to 12 servings.*

VIENNESE PEACH TART
(Austria)

CRUST:

½ cup butter or margarine
¼ cup confectioners' sugar
1 cup sifted enriched flour

Cream butter until soft. Add sugar gradually, continuing to cream. Blend in flour to make a soft dough. Pat evenly into 12-inch pizza pan, covering bottom and sides. Bake at 350° F for 20 minutes.

The statue attached to the café Zwirina commemorates Kolschitsky, Vienna's first coffeehouse proprietor.

FILLING:

1 tablespoon cornstarch
2 tablespoons sugar
¼ teaspoon mace
½ cup orange juice

½ cup red-currant jelly,
melted
8 large fresh peaches
(about)

Combine cornstarch, sugar, and mace. Add orange juice. Cook over hot water, stirring, until thick and clear. Stir in melted currant jelly. Cool slightly. Peel and slice peaches. Arrange in single layer in baked shell. Spoon glaze evenly over peaches. Chill. Garnish with whipped cream. *Makes 6 to 8 servings.*

VIENNESE STRIESEL
(Austria)

1 package dry active yeast
or 1 cake compressed
yeast
¼ cup warm (not hot)
water
½ cup milk
¼ cup sugar
1 teaspoon salt
2 tablespoons melted
shortening
2¾ to 3 cups flour, sifted
1 egg

¼ cup seedless raisins
¼ cup chopped, candied
cherries
2 tablespoons chopped,
candied orange rind
⅛ teaspoon mace
½ cup confectioners'
sugar
1 tablespoon top milk or
cream
¼ cup chopped nuts

Sprinkle dry yeast into warm (not hot) water. (Crumble compressed yeast into lukewarm water.) Stir until dissolved. Scald milk. Pour into large mixing bowl or into large bowl of electric mixer. Add sugar, salt, and shortening. Cool until just warm. Stir in 1 cup flour. Mix in dissolved yeast. Add egg and beat hard. (Egg may be beaten separately and then added to batter.) Stir in raisins, cherries, orange rind, and mace. Stir in 1½ cups flour. Sprinkle 2 tablespoons of the remaining ¼ cup flour on breadboard or pastry cloth. Turn dough out on flour and knead, adding more flour as needed to make a soft dough. Knead until dough is smooth and satiny (about 5 minutes). Shape into smooth ball. Wash mixing bowl and grease lightly. Press top of dough ball into bowl, then turn dough over. Cover and let rise until doubled (about 2¼ hours). Punch down. Divide into 9 pieces. Shape each piece into a ball. Cover and let rest 5 minutes. Roll each piece under the hands to form strands about 15 inches long. Weave 4 strands into a loose braid. Lay the strands on a lightly greased baking sheet, overlapping them at the center. Braid from the center toward each end. With the sides of the hands make a "trench" down the center of this braid. Now braid the next 3 strands loosely, again braiding from the center toward each end. Lay this braid on top of the first one, placing it in the "trench." Last of all, twist the 2 remaining strands loosely around each other. Lay this twist on top of the loaf, bringing the ends of the twist down over the ends of the loaf. Tuck the ends of the twist under the loaf. Cover and let rise until doubled (about 1½ hours). Bake in moderate oven (350° F), 40 to 45 minutes. Remove from baking sheet to rack. When cool, make frosting by mixing confectioners' sugar with milk or cream. Spread on loaf. Sprinkle with chopped almonds or walnuts.

COFFEE BREAD
(Belgium)

1 package dry active yeast	⅓ cup butter or margarine
1 cup warm water	7 cups sifted enriched flour
1 cup milk	(about)
½ cup sugar	1 cup seedless raisins
1 teaspoon salt	2 eggs
1 teaspoon ground cardamom	1 egg, beaten
	1 tablespoon water

Soften yeast in water. Scald milk. Add sugar, salt, cardamom and butter or margarine. Cool to lukewarm. Add 2 cups flour and beat well. Add softened yeast, raisins and 2 eggs. Add enough more flour to make a soft dough. Turn out on lightly floured board or pastry cloth and knead until smooth and satiny. Place in greased bowl, cover and let rise in warm place until doubled (about 1½ hours). When light, punch down. Divide dough into 2 equal portions. Let rest 10 minutes. Shape each portion into round loaf. Place in greased 9-inch-round pans. Let rise until doubled (about 1 hour). Mix egg and water. Brush lightly over tops of loaves. Bake in moderate oven (375°), 40 to 45 minutes. *Makes 2 round loaves.*

KOLACHKY
(Bohemia)

½ cup lukewarm milk
½ cup sugar
1 teaspoon salt
2 envelopes dry active yeast
½ cup warm water (105°–115° F)

2 eggs, unbeaten
½ cup soft shortening
4½ to 5 cups enriched flour (measure according to directions on package)
Cottage Cheese Filling*

Combine milk, sugar, and salt. Sprinkle yeast on warm water. Let stand 5 minutes. Stir well and add to milk mixture. Stir in eggs and shortening. Add enough flour to make a soft dough, first with spoon and then with hand. Knead until smooth and elastic. Cover. Let rise in warm place until double in bulk. Punch down. Let rise again until almost double (30 to 45 minutes). Shape into 2-inch balls. Cover. Let rise again until light (15 to 30 minutes). Make a depression in center of each and fill with Cottage Cheese Filling. Place on greased baking sheet. Bake in hot oven (400° F), 20 to 25 minutes. *Makes about 2½ dozen.*

COTTAGE CHEESE FILLING*

1½ cups cottage cheese
2 egg yolks
½ teaspoon mace
1 tablespoon grated lemon
peel

1 tablespoon lemon juice
1 tablespoon sugar
½ cup seedless raisins

Combine all ingredients; mix well.

KING'S RING
(Brazil)

⅔ cup milk
¾ cup sugar
1 teaspoon salt
6 tablespoons shortening
2 packages dry active yeast
⅔ cup warm water

3 eggs, beaten
7 cups all-purpose flour
Cinnamon sugar
1 cup diced, candied fruit
1 cup chopped Brazil nuts

Scald milk. Stir in sugar, salt, and shortening. Cool to lukewarm. Dissolve yeast in water; add milk mixture. Stir in eggs,
then 3 cups flour. Beat smooth. Stir in enough remaining
flour to make soft dough. Knead until smooth and elastic.
Put in well-greased bowl, turning greased side to top. Cover;
let rise in warm place until doubled (about 1½ hours).
Punch down. Put on floured board; divide. Roll each half
into 14×12-inch oblong. Brush with melted butter. Sprinkle
oblongs with cinnamon sugar, candied fruit, and nuts. Hide
2 tiny, foil-wrapped trinkets in dough. Roll into two ropes
1½ inches in diameter. Form each into ring in greased 10-
inch ring molds. Brush with butter. Cover; let rise until
doubled (about 1 hour). Bake in oven (375° F) for ½ hour.
Cool. Frost and decorate. Makes 2 rings.

COFFEE TWIST
(Denmark)

1 package active dry yeast
or 1 cake compressed
yeast
¼ cup warm water
½ cup milk
¼ cup sugar
1 teaspoon salt
2 tablespoons melted
shortening

2¾ to 3 cups flour, sifted
1 egg
3 tablespoons sugar
½ teaspoon cinnamon
1 tablespoon soft
margarine or butter
Honey Glaze*
¼ cup slivered, blanched
almonds

Sprinkle dry yeast into warm water or crumble compressed yeast into lukewarm water. Stir until dissolved. Scald milk. Pour into large mixing bowl or into large bowl of electric mixer. Add sugar, salt, and shortening. Cool until just warm. Stir in 1 cup flour. Mix in dissolved yeast. Add egg and beat hard. (Egg may be beaten separately and then added to batter.) Stir in 1½ cups flour. Sprinkle 2 tablespoons of the remaining ¼ cup flour on breadboard or pastry cloth. Turn dough out on flour and knead, adding more flour as needed to make a soft dough. Knead until dough is smooth and satiny (about 5 minutes). Shape into smooth balls. Wash mixing bowl and grease lightly. Press top of dough ball into bowl, then turn dough over. Cover and let rise until doubled (about 2 hours). Punch down. Cover and let rest 5 to 10 minutes. When dough has doubled, punch down. Shape into ball. Cover and let rest 5 minutes.

While dough rests, mix sugar and cinnamon. Flatten ball of dough, then roll out to form long, narrow sheet about 6 inches wide and ¼ inch thick. Spread with soft margarine or butter. Sprinkle with sugar-cinnamon mixture. Roll up to make long, slender roll. Seal edge by pressing firmly. Twist roll by pushing ends in opposite directions. Lift to lightly greased baking sheet and shape into a large "pretzel." Tuck ends of roll under edge of pretzel to keep dough from untwisting. Cover and let rise until doubled (about 1 hour). Bake in moderate oven (350° F), 25 to 30 minutes. While Coffee Twist bakes, make Honey Glaze. Brush hot glaze over twist as soon as it comes from oven. Sprinkle with slivered almonds. Remove from baking sheet to cooling rack.

HONEY GLAZE*

2 tablespoons sugar
¼ cup honey
1 tablespoon margarine or butter

Measure ingredients into small saucepan. Bring to boil, stirring constantly. While still hot, brush on baked Coffee Twist.

CREAM CONES
(Denmark)

⅓ cup butter or margarine   4 egg whites
⅓ cup sugar   Strawberry jam
½ cup sifted all-purpose   ½ cup heavy cream
   flour

Melt butter. Stir in sugar and flour. Stir until smooth. Beat egg whites stiff. Fold in. Drop from measuring tablespoon onto hot, well-greased baking sheet, spacing well apart. Bake only 2 or 3 at a time. Spread each mound into paper-thin oblong about 4 inches by 5 inches. Bake at 400° F for 5 minutes or until deep golden brown. Quickly remove and roll into cones while hot. Continue until batter is used. Fill bottom of cooled cones with strawberry jam. Whip cream. Fill large ends of cones with whipped cream forced through pastry tube. Store unused cones in tightly covered metal container to prevent softening. *Makes 10 cones.*

SCONES
(Scotland)

3 cups biscuit mix	1 cup milk
5 tablespoons sugar,	¼ teaspoon cinnamon
divided	1 tablespoon melted butter
½ cup seedless raisins	1 tablespoon heavy cream

Combine biscuit mix and 2 tablespoons of sugar; stir in raisins. Add milk slowly, mixing lightly with a fork. Roll out on lightly floured board about ¾ inch thick. Cut with a 1-inch cookie cutter into small biscuits. Bake in hot oven (425° F), 12 to 15 minutes or until lightly browned. Combine remaining sugar and cinnamon; blend in melted butter and cream. Brush biscuit tops with this mixture. Place under broiler, about 4 inches from source of heat, and broil until topping is bubbly and lightly browned. Serve hot, with butter and jam or marmalade. *Makes about 24.*

BRIOCHES
(France)

1 cup milk, scalded	½ cup melted butter or
6 tablespoons sugar	margarine
1 teaspoon salt	2 eggs, beaten
2 compressed yeast cakes	5½ to 6 cups sifted flour
¼ cup lukewarm water	Egg-Yolk Glaze*

Combine scalded milk, sugar, and salt. Stir until sugar dissolves. Dissolve yeast in lukewarm water. Combine yeast and milk mixture. Add butter or margarine and eggs; mix well. Add flour gradually until a soft dough is formed. Knead slightly. Cover and let rise in warm place until doubled in bulk. Knead slightly again. Make 24 balls of dough about 2 inches in diameter, using ⅔ of dough. Place in greased muffin pans or deep-fluted tart-shell pans. Form remaining dough into 24 small balls about ¾ inch in diameter and set firmly on larger balls. Cover; let rise in warm place until double in bulk. Brush with Egg-Yolk Glaze. Bake in moderate oven (350° F) about 20 minutes or until deep golden brown. *Makes 2 dozen brioches.*

EGG-YOLK GLAZE*

1 egg yolk, beaten
1 tablespoon heavy cream
1 teaspoon sugar

Combine and mix well. Brush on brioches with pastry brush just before baking.

CROISSANTS
(France)

2 packages active dry yeast   *1 egg*
½ cup warm (not hot)   *2 tablespoons sugar*
   water (110°–115° F)   *5 cups biscuit mix*
½ cup milk, scalded   *⅔ cup butter or margarine*

Dissolve yeast in warm water. Cool milk to lukewarm and add to dissolved yeast with egg, sugar, and biscuit mix. Mix thoroughly to a stiff dough. Turn dough out on board, well dusted with biscuit mix. Knead until smooth. Roll into square ¼ inch thick. Dot with ⅓ cup butter, leaving 2-inch margin. Fold in half and seal edges. Dot with remaining ⅓ cup butter, leaving 2-inch margin. Fold in half, seal edges. Roll into square ⅓ inch thick. Fold in half, then in half again. Roll out. Fold and roll 3 times more. Place in greased bowl. Cover and let stand 20 minutes. Roll into 16-inch circle and cut into 16 wedges. Roll up each wedge, starting at wide end, stretching a little as you roll. Turn ends in to form crescents. Paint each crescent twice with a blend of egg yolk and water. Cover and let rise until it doubles. Bake on ungreased cookie sheet in hot oven (400° F), 12 to 15 minutes. *Makes 16 Croissants.*

COFFEE BREAD
(France)

2 *packages yeast,*
  compressed or dry
¼ *cup water (lukewarm*
  for compressed yeast,
  warm for dry)
½ *cup milk*
⅓ *cup sugar*
1 *teaspoon salt*
⅔ *cup melted butter or*
  margarine

4 *cups sifted enriched*
  flour (about)
1½ *teaspoons vanilla*
  extract
4 *eggs, beaten*
Confectioners'-sugar icing
Chopped, blanched
  almonds
Candied fruit pieces

Soften yeast in water. Scald milk; add sugar, salt, and butter or margarine. Cool to lukewarm. Add flour to make a thick batter. Mix well. Add softened yeast, vanilla extract, and eggs. Beat well. Add sufficient flour to make a stiff batter. Beat thoroughly until smooth. Cover and let rise in warm place until bubbly (about 1 hour). Stir down. Turn batter into well-greased, 10-inch tube pan or two well-greased, 1¼-

quart ring molds. Let rise until doubled (about 45 minutes for tube pan and about 30 minutes for ring molds). Bake in moderate oven (350° F) about 35 minutes for tube pan and 25 to 30 minutes for ring molds. Remove from pan and cool. Drizzle with confectioners'-sugar icing and decorate with almonds and candied fruit. *Makes 1 large or 2 medium-sized coffee breads.*

LEBKUCHEN
(Germany)

½ cup honey
½ cup molasses
¾ cup firmly packed brown sugar
1 egg
1 teaspoon grated lemon peel
1 tablespoon lemon juice
2¾ cups sifted enriched flour
½ teaspoon baking soda

½ teaspoon salt
1 teaspoon each: nutmeg, cloves, cinnamon, allspice
¾ cup finely diced, candied citron
½ cup finely chopped nuts
Blanched almonds
Candied cherries
Glaze

Put first 3 ingredients in saucepan. Bring to boil, stirring until sugar is dissolved. Cool. Stir in egg, lemon peel, and juice. Add sifted dry ingredients, citron, and chopped nuts; mix well. Chill overnight. Roll out to ¼ inch thickness; cut into squares or oblongs. Put on greased cookie sheets. Garnish with almonds and candied cherries. Bake in oven (400° F) 10 to 12 minutes. Frost with thin icing, if desired. *Makes about 2 dozen 2-inch-square cookies.*

STOLLEN
(Germany)

1 package dry active yeast
or 1 cake compressed
yeast
¼ cup warm water
½ cup milk
¼ cup sugar
1 teaspoon salt
2 teaspoons melted
shortening
2¾ to 3 cups flour, sifted
1 egg
½ cup chopped, blanched
almonds

¼ cup finely cut, candied
citron
¼ cup finely cut, candied
cherries
1 teaspoon grated lemon
rind
1 tablespoon soft
margarine or butter
2 tablespoons sugar
½ teaspoon cinnamon
Frosting*

Sprinkle dry yeast into warm water or crumble compressed yeast into lukewarm water. Stir until dissolved. Scald milk. Pour into large mixing bowl or into large bowl of electric mixer. Add sugar, salt, and shortening. Cool until just warm. Stir in 1 cup flour. Mix in dissolved yeast. Add egg and beat hard. (Egg may be beaten separately and then added to batter.) Stir in almonds, citron, cherries, and lemon rind. Stir in 1½ cups flour. Sprinkle 2 tablespoons of the remaining ¼ cup flour on breadboard or pastry cloth. Turn dough out on flour and knead, adding more flour as needed to make a soft dough. Knead until dough is smooth and satiny (about 5 minutes). Shape into smooth ball. Wash mixing bowl and grease lightly. Press top of dough ball into bowl, then turn dough over. Cover and let rise until doubled (about 2¼ hours). Punch down. Cover and let rest 5 to 10 minutes. With palms of hands press dough into oval shape a scant ½ inch thick. Spread half of oval with soft margarine or butter. Mix sugar and cinnamon. Sprinkle over margarine or butter. Fold the unspread half, lengthwise, over sugar and cinnamon, making edges even. Lift to lightly greased baking sheet. Curve the ends slightly. Press down the folded edge (not the open edge). This helps the loaf keep its shape as it rises and bakes. Cover and let rise until doubled (about 1¼ hours). Bake in moderate oven (350° F), 30 to 35 minutes. Remove from baking sheet. When cool, frost and decorate. *Makes 1 loaf.*

FROSTING*

¾ cup sifted confectioners' sugar
1 tablespoon top milk or cream

3 candied cherries, sliced
2 tablespoons chopped or slivered almonds

Mix sugar and milk or cream to make a smooth, thick frosting that will just pour. Pour it over top of loaf, letting frosting drip down sides. Decorate with sliced cherries and sprinkle with almonds.

COFFEE BREAD
(Greece)

1 package dry active yeast or 1 cake compressed yeast
¼ cup warm water
½ cup milk
¼ cup sugar
1 teaspoon salt
2 tablespoons melted shortening

2¾ to 3 cups flour, sifted
1 egg
½ cup currants
¾ cup confectioners' sugar
1 tablespoon milk or cream
15 blanched almonds
¼ cup sliced, candied cherries

Sprinkle dry yeast into warm water or crumble compressed yeast into lukewarm water. Stir until dissolved. Scald milk.

Pour into large mixing bowl or into large bowl of electric mixer. Add sugar, salt, and shortening. Cool until just warm. Stir in 1 cup flour. Mix in dissolved yeast. Add egg and beat hard. (Egg may be beaten separately and then added to batter.) Stir in currants. Stir in 1½ cups flour. Sprinkle 2 tablespoons of the remaining ¼ cup flour on breadboard or pastry cloth. Turn dough out on flour; knead, adding more flour as needed to make a soft dough. Knead until dough is smooth and satiny (about 5 minutes). Shape into smooth ball. Wash mixing bowl and grease lightly. Press top of dough ball into bowl, then turn dough over. Cover and let rise until doubled (about 2 hours). Punch down. Divide dough into 3 equal parts. Shape each part into smooth ball. Place balls on lightly greased baking sheet so that they form a three-leafed clover, about ½ inch apart. Cover and let rise until doubled (about 1 hour). Bake in moderate oven (350° F), 40 to 45 minutes. Remove from baking sheet and cool on rack. When cool, mix confectioners' sugar and milk or cream to make a soft frosting. Pour over each of the 3 loaves, letting frosting drip down sides. Arrange almonds and sliced cherries in three-petaled flower shapes on frosting. Cut into thin slices.

SODA BREAD
(Ireland)

2 cups all-purpose flour	½ cup light, seedless
¾ teaspoon baking soda	raisins
½ teaspoon salt	1 tablespoon caraway seeds
1 tablespoon sugar	¼ cup vinegar
6 tablespoons shortening	½ cup milk

Mix and sift flour, baking soda, salt, and sugar. Cut in shortening with two knives or pastry blender. Stir in raisins and caraway seeds. Combine vinegar and milk. Add to flour mixture and blend with a fork. Turn into greased 8-inch, layer-cake pan 1½ inches deep; pat smooth. Bake in moderate oven (375° F), 30 minutes or until done. This recipe may be doubled and baked in a greased 1½-quart casserole for a longer time—about 1 hour. *Makes 1 loaf.*

COFFEE BREAD
(Italy)

2 packages dry active yeast
½ cup warm water
½ cup firmly packed
    brown sugar
½ cup butter or
    margarine, melted
2 unbeaten eggs
3 unbeaten egg yolks

1 teaspoon salt
4 to 4½ cups all-purpose
    flour
½ cup raisins
½ cup chopped, candied
    fruit
Glaze*

Soften yeast in warm water. Combine in mixing bowl brown sugar, butter, eggs, egg yolks, and salt. Stir in the yeast. Add flour to form a stiff dough. Knead on floured surface until smooth and satiny, about 5 minutes. Add raisins and candied fruit; knead until fruit is evenly distributed, about 5 minutes. Divide dough into 2 parts. Form into balls and place on well-greased cookie sheet. Cover. Let rise in warm place (85° to 90° F) until doubled in size, 2 to 3 hours. Brush with glaze. If desired, make a deep cross on top with a sharp knife and sprinkle with coarse, crystallized sugar. Bake at 325° F for 35 to 45 minutes. *Makes 2 round loaves.*

GLAZE*

1 unbeaten egg yolk
2 teaspoons flour

2 teaspoons sugar
2 teaspoons water

Combine egg yolk, flour, sugar, and water to form a paste.

A view of the famed Caffè Quadri, still situated on the
Piazza San Marco in Venice.

PIZZA RUSTICA
(*Italy*)

PIE CRUST:

2 cups biscuit mix   3 tablespoons shortening
½ teaspoon salt   ⅔ cup milk
¼ teaspoon coarse, ground
pepper

Combine biscuit mix, salt, and pepper. Cut in shortening
until mixture is crumbly. Add milk; mix well. Roll out to
make top and bottom crust for 10-inch pie.

FILLING:

1 pound sweet Italian
sausage
¼ cup water
3 eggs, well beaten
¼ teaspoon coarse, ground
pepper

¼ cup grated Parmesan
cheese
1 pound ricotta cheese
½ pound mozzarella
cheese, sliced thin

Remove sausage from casing and break up into small pieces. Put in frying pan with ¼ cup water. Cover and simmer slowly until lightly browned. Blend beaten eggs, pepper, grated Parmesan cheese, and ricotta. Add sausage. Spoon into pastry-lined, 10-inch piepan. Top with mozzarella slices. Cover with pastry and flute edges. Pierce top with fork. Bake in hot oven (425° F) until golden brown (about 25 minutes). Serve in small wedges, hot or cold. *Makes 12 servings.*

SICILIAN CREAM CAKE
(Italy)

1 package (2 layers)
baker's spongecake
1 pound ricotta (Italian
cottage cheese)
½ cup sugar

2 squares (1 ounce each)
unsweetened chocolate,
grated
Few drops almond extract

Split cake layers crosswise to make 4 layers. Combine ricotta and sugar. Mix thoroughly. Stir in grated chocolate and flavoring. Spread 3 cake layers with cheese mixture and stack. Top with remaining layer. Chill. Frost top and sides with Mocha Frosting.* Decorate with chocolate curls. *Makes 8 servings.*

COFFEE BREAD
(Norway)

2 packages dry active yeast
½ cup warm water (110°–115° F)
2 cups milk, scalded
½ cup vanilla sugar
2 teaspoons salt
¾ teaspoon ground cardamom
8 cups sifted all-purpose flour
½ cup butter or margarine, melted
1¼ cups butter or margarine
1 cup diced, mixed glacé fruit
1 cup raisins
Milk

Soften yeast in warm water. Cool milk and add to yeast along with sugar, salt, and cardamom. Stir in 4 cups of the sifted flour and beat until the batter falls in sheets from a spoon. Cool melted butter or margarine and beat it into the yeast batter. Gradually add remaining flour and knead until smooth and elastic, about 8 minutes. Shape into a ball. Place in a greased bowl. Cover and let rise until double in bulk, about 1 hour. Punch down dough. Place on a pastry board. Cut butter or margarine into small pieces and knead it into the dough. Add glacé fruit and raisins; knead until well distributed. Shape into two loaves. Place each in a greased 9×5×3-inch bread pan. Brush tops of loaves with milk. Cover and let rise until double in bulk. Bake in a preheated moderate oven (375° F), 30 minutes or until lightly browned. *Makes 2 loaves.*

KULICH
(*Russia*)

1 package dry active yeast
or 1 cake compressed
yeast
¼ cup warm water
½ cup milk
¼ cup sugar
1 teaspoon salt
2 tablespoons melted
shortening

2¾ cups sifted enriched
1 egg
¼ cup raisins
¼ cup chopped almonds
1 teaspoon grated lemon
rind
Frosting*

Sprinkle dry yeast into warm water or crumble compressed yeast into lukewarm water. Stir until dissolved. Scald milk. Pour into large mixing bowl or into large bowl of electric mixer. Add sugar, salt, and shortening. Cool until just warm. Stir in 1 cup flour. Mix in dissolved yeast. Add egg and beat hard. (Egg may be beaten separately and then added to batter.) Stir in raisins, almonds and lemon rind. Stir in 1½ cups flour. Sprinkle 2 tablespoons of flour on breadboard or pastry cloth. Turn dough out on flour and knead, adding more flour as needed to make a soft dough. Knead until dough is smooth and satiny (about 5 minutes). Shape into smooth ball. Wash mixing bowl and grease lightly. Press top of dough ball into bowl, then turn dough over. Cover and let rise until doubled (about 2 hours). Punch down. Divide into halves. Shape into balls. Press each ball into greased one-pint can (such as fruit or juice cans), or one-pound coffee or shortening cans. Cover and let rise until doubled (about 1¼ hours). Bake in moderate oven (350° F), 30 to 35 minutes. Turn out of cans at once. When cool, frost tops with Frosting and decorate with almonds and sliced, candied cherries, or sprinkle with small, colored candies.

FROSTING*

½ cup sifted confectioners'   2 tablespoons slivered
  sugar   almonds
2 teaspoons top milk or   2 candied cherries, sliced
  cream

Mix sugar and milk to make smooth, thin frosting. Pour over tops of loaves. Decorate with almonds and sliced cherries. To serve: cut slices from top to bottom so each slice has a bit of frosting.

PASKHA
(Russia)

¾ pound cream cheese   ½ cup mixed diced
¼ pound (1 stick) sweet   candied peels
  butter   1½ cups seedless raisins
½ cup sour cream   1 envelope unflavored
½ cup sugar   gelatin
1 cup chopped almonds   ¼ cup cold water

Mash cream cheese. Beat in butter, sour cream and sugar; beat until well blended and creamy. Add almonds, candied peels and raisins. Soften gelatin in cold water. Dissolve over hot water. Add; mix well. Turn into oiled 4-cup mold. Chill. When ready to serve, unmold onto serving plate. Decorate with additional almonds and candied peels arranged in the form of an equal-armed cross. *Makes 8 to 10 servings.*

SHORTBREAD
(Scotland)

1 cup butter or margarine
½ cup sugar
2 cups flour, sifted

Cream butter or margarine thoroughly. Add sugar gradually while continuing to cream. Add flour gradually. Shape into two round cakes, about 8 inches in diameter. Flute edges. Prick surface with tines of fork. Place on greased cookie sheet. Bake in hot oven (450° F), 8 to 10 minutes, or until golden brown. Cut in wedges to serve. *Makes 8 servings.*

BRAZO DE GITANO
(Spain)

⅓ cup granulated sugar
3 eggs, separated
½ cup sifted cake flour
¼ teaspoon salt
½ teaspoon baking powder
1 teaspoon grated lemon
    rind
2 tablespoons boiling water

¼ cup chopped
    maraschino cherries
    (about 10 cherries)
⅓ cup orange marmalade
½ cup heavy cream,
    whipped
Confectioners' sugar

Beat sugar and egg yolks until thick and lemon-colored. Sift together: flour, salt, and baking powder; gradually beat into egg mixture. Add lemon rind and boiling water; beat until smooth. Beat egg whites until stiff, but not dry; fold into egg-yolk mixture. Turn into greased 9-inch-square pan. Bake in moderate-hot oven (375° F), 20 to 25 minutes, or until cake tests done. Remove from pan immediately. Turn cake onto towel sprinkled with confectioners' sugar. Roll up jelly-roll fashion. Remove from towel and cool. Combine cherries and marmalade. Unroll cake and spread with cherry mixture;

top with whipped cream and reroll. Sprinkle with confectioners' sugar and garnish with additional cherries, as desired. Refrigerate until served. *Makes one 9-inch roll.*

PALMA BISCUITS
(Spain)

⅓ cup butter or margarine
½ cup sugar
1 egg
1 tablespoon grated lemon rind
1½ cups sifted all-purpose flour
9 glacé cherries, finely chopped
9 glacé cherries, cut in half
18 whole filberts

Cream butter and sugar. Mix in egg and lemon rind. Mix in flour and chopped cherries. Roll out between waxed paper to ¼ inch thickness. Cut out with floured 2-inch cookie cutter. Place on greased cookie sheets. Top each biscuit with cherry half and filbert. Bake in moderate oven (375° F), 8 to 10 minutes, or until golden. Sprinkle with sifted confectioners' sugar, if desired. *Makes 1½ dozen.*

LUSSEKAKE
(Sweden)

2 tablespoons boiling water
½ teaspoon crumbled saffron threads
1 package dry active yeast
¼ cup warm water (110° F)
½ cup butter or margarine
⅓ cup sugar
1 teaspoon salt
1 cup milk, scalded
3½ to 4 cups sifted all-purpose flour
1 egg, well beaten

Pour boiling water on saffron and let stand. Add yeast to ¼ cup of warm water, stirring until dissolved. Let stand 5 to 10 minutes. Meanwhile put butter, sugar, and salt in large bowl, add scalded milk and stir until butter melts. Let stand until lukewarm and then blend in one cup of the flour. Beat smooth. Add yeast and mix well. Add about half the remaining flour and beat smooth. Beat in saffron-water mixture and egg. Add enough remaining flour to make a soft dough. Turn out on floured board. Let "rest" 5 to 10 minutes. Knead until smooth and elastic. Place in greased bowl, cover and let rise in warm place until doubled. Punch down. Make each bun with 2 strips of dough, 4 inches long and ¼ inch in diameter. Form each strip into an S, coiling the ends snail fashion. Place one diagonally across the other, pressing together in center. Place a raisin in center of each coil. Cover and let rise until doubled. Bake at 375° F for 15 to 20 minutes. *Makes 24 buns.*

COFFEE RING
(Sweden)

1 package dry active yeast
1 teaspoon sugar
¼ cup warm water
1 cup milk, scalded
7 tablespoons butter or
    margarine, melted
1 teaspoon salt
½ teaspoon cardamom
½ cup sugar
3 egg yolks, slightly
    beaten

½ cup chopped citron
5½ cups flour, sifted
½ cup light-brown sugar,
    firmly packed
½ teaspoon cinnamon
¼ teaspoon ginger
Confectioners'-Sugar
    Frosting*

Dissolve yeast and 1 teaspoon sugar in warm water. Combine milk and 5 tablespoons butter or margarine; cool to lukewarm. Add salt, cardamom, ½ cup sugar, egg yolks, citron, and yeast mixture. Beat well. Gradually add flour to make soft dough; knead until smooth. Place in greased bowl, turning once to coat top lightly with shortening. Cover. Let rise in warm place until light and double in bulk, about 1 hour. Punch down. Divide in half. Turn out on floured board. Roll each into rectangle ½ inch thick. Brush with remaining melted butter or margarine. Sprinkle each with brown sugar, cinnamon, and ginger. Roll as for jellyroll. Place on greased baking sheet. Bring ends of roll together to make ring. Press ends firmly together. With scissors, make cuts two thirds of the way through the ring at one-inch intervals. Turn each on its side. Let rise until double in bulk, about 45 minutes. Bake at 350° F for 30 to 35 minutes. Cool slightly. Frost with Confectioners'-Sugar Frosting. *Makes 2 rings.*

CONFECTIONERS'-SUGAR FROSTING*

2 *tablespoons milk*
1 *cup confectioners' sugar, sifted*

Gradually add milk to sugar. Beat until smooth. *Makes Frosting for 2 rings.*

VETEBROD
(Sweden)

1 *package dry active yeast*
¼ *cup warm water (110°–115° F)*
1⅓ *cups lukewarm milk*
1 *egg*
½ *cup sugar*
½ *teaspoon salt*
4½ *cups sifted enriched flour (about)*

1 *teaspoon powdered cardamom*
⅓ *cup soft butter or margarine*
1 *beaten egg*
Slivered, blanched almonds

Add yeast to warm water and stir until dissolved. Add lukewarm milk. Beat egg and sugar together. Add milk mixture, salt, and some of the flour. Stir to mix. Add cardamom and sufficient flour to make a soft dough. Knead vigorously until thoroughly mixed. Add butter. Knead until dough no longer sticks to sides of bowl. Cover; let rise in warm place (85° F) until doubled in bulk. Punch down. Divide into 3 equal portions. Shape each portion into a long strand. Braid strands to form a loaf. Cover; let rise again until doubled in bulk. Brush with slightly beaten egg. Sprinkle with slivered blanched almonds. Bake in moderate oven (350° F) about 30 minutes or until golden brown and done. Cool, then frost if desired with Confectioners'-Sugar Frosting. *Makes 1 coffee bread.*

SCHLOSS HERBLINGEN APPLE PIE
(*Switzerland*)

¼ cup butter or margarine
1½ cups sifted all-purpose flour
3 tablespoons cold water
1 tablespoon crushed, toasted almonds
1 tablespoon fine, dry bread crumbs

4 cups thinly sliced, tart apples
2 eggs
2 egg yolks
2 cups heavy cream
¾ cup sugar, divided
2 tablespoons butter or margarine, melted

Cut butter into flour with pastry blender or 2 knives. Add cold water gradually, mixing with fork, until pastry gathers around fork. Roll out on lightly floured board ⅛ inch thick. Line deep, 10-inch piepan; trim edge. Sprinkle almonds and crumbs over pastry in bottom of piepan. Arrange apple slices in piepan, layering evenly; do not heap. Bake at 350° F for 5 minutes. Meanwhile, combine eggs and yolks. Beat slightly. Add cream and ½ cup sugar. Stir until sugar dissolves. Pour half of this mixture over apples. Bake until firm (about ½ hour). Pour in remaining mixture. Bake again until knife inserted near edge comes out clean (about ½ hour). Remove pie from oven. Pour 2 tablespoons melted butter evenly over top. Sprinkle with remaining sugar. Return to oven. Bake 5 minutes longer, or until top is crusty and golden. Let pie cool somewhat before cutting.

A street coffee vendor of the 1670s in Holland. Two cents per cup, including sugar.

Index